# LIFE • PASSION • DUTY

# THE Nnaabagereka

## QUEEN SYLVIA NAGGINDA LUSWATA

## AN AUTOBIOGRAPHY

Scripture quotations are taken from the *Holy Bible*, New Living Translation, copyright © 1996, 2004, 2015 by Tyndale House Foundation. Used by permission of Tyndale House Publishers, Inc., Carol Stream, Illinois 60188. All rights reserved.

Published by Eagle's Wings Press
sempebwa.com
connect@sempebwa.com

Publishing services by:
EVANGELISTA MEDIA & CONSULTING
evangelistamedia.com
publisher@evangelistamedia.com

Cover design by Buyungo Bryan Bedford
Photography by Giulio Molfese
Hair by Afros and Mo
Make-up by Mona Faces

ISBN: 978-1-7327572-9-5

1 2 3 4 5 6 / 26 25 24 23

# DEDICATED TO

Katrina-Sarah Ssangalyambogo
Jade Catherine Nakato
Jasmine Rebecca Babirye

# ACKNOWLEDGEMENTS

I would like to thank His Majesty Kabaka Ronald Mutebi for his invaluable support. When he chose me to be his wife, I became the Nnaabagereka of Buganda Kingdom, a position that has given me a wide platform and latitude to contribute to the development of our country through support to children, youth, and women in Uganda.

To our children: Junju, Joan and Vicky for accepting me to be your mummy and for the times we've shared—I love you! Ssanga, Jade, and Jasmine for giving me encouragement and love to keep writing.

To my grandparents, Taata and Maama, the late Nelson and Catherine Sebugwawo. Their nurturing is the strong foundation I still stand on, now sixty years running.

My late father John Luswata for the love he showed me, in spite of the often impossible limitations.

My mother Rebecca Musoke for her inner strength and resilience, which has undoubtedly rubbed off on me. I remember you saying, 'Sylvia, you have to work really hard because no one else will do it for you'. I heard you, Mum.

Daddy Maxwell Codjoe for embracing me as one of your own and showing me that caring for others leaves an everlasting mark.

Mummy Edith Luswata for your enduring efforts at being a supportive mother.

My sisters and brothers Barbara, Juliet, and Nelson for the glorious childhood days together. To John Jr. the gentle soul. Rueben and Monique for your never-ending support and love.

*Ssengas ne ba taata* (my paternal aunties and uncles) for embracing me as your daughter, sister, and friend in the absence of my biological parents. Ssenga Cate Bamundaga, you have been simply amazing!

Cate Bwete, I love you dearly for being such a true sister and confidant. Fred Lutalo for sticking with me and believing in me through it all. Thank you Sarah Kiyingi for being a true friend and confidant. And to Aunt Joyce Sebugwawo for always looking out for me and being the big cheerleader you have been.

My office support staff led by Juliet Ssenteza have been an incredible family that I never had. Without you, I would not have been able to do as much as what we've done together. Thank you so much Susan Lubega, Hadijja Nabisubi, Annette Nanyonga, Hadijja Sendikwanawa, and Gorette Namagga. Herbert Ssemutenga, you've been simply outstanding—thank you.

The Nnabagereka Development Foundation—trustees, governance board, and the secretariat. I have been blessed to work with some of the most intelligent and professional people of high integrity for so many years. To the current members of the Board of Trustees Mrs Judy Kamanyi, Mrs Maria Kiwanuka, and Mr John Katende. Special thanks to Judith and Maria for serving the foundation since its inception in 2000. Judith, thank you for always being available to bounce ideas off and to spruce up our written communications.

To all Board members past and present: H.E. Thelma Awori, Mrs Sarah Bagalaaliwo, Mr Arthur Bagunywa, Justice Solome Bossa, Ambassador Klaus Holderbaum, Princess Sarah Kagere, Mr Abdu Kagga, Mr Mohammed Kakiika, Mrs Judith Kamanyi, Mr John Katende, Mr Robert Kiggundu, Honourable Maria Kiwanuka, Ms Elizabeth Lwanga, Ambassador Nimisha Madhvani, Mrs Sarah Mangale (RIP), Mr James Mugabi, Mrs Beatrice N. Mugambe, Honourable Apollonia Mugumbya, Dr Moses Musaazi-Kiiza (RIP), Mrs Mary Mutyaba (RIP), Princess Agnes Nabaloga, Dr Josephine Namboze Kiggundu, Ms Sauda Namyaalo, Dr Maria Nassali, Mr Roscoe Nsubuga, Ms Maria Prean, Justice Julia Sebutinde, Dr Jeff Sebuyira-Mukasa, Mr Aloysius Semmanda, Dr Lydia Ssebuyira, Dr Olive Ssentumbwe-Mugisa, Mr Jameel Verjee, and Prince David Wassajja. To Andrew Mukiibi for steering the secretariat against many odds; you are a true professional.

I am grateful to Dr Margret Sekiide, Dr Sarah Nkonge, Dr Maria Nassali, and Mrs Susan Busulwa Lubega for their tenacity and assiduously supporting me in establishing the Nnabagereka Nagginda Women's Fund or NNWF.

The men and women who work diligently for the good and love of Buganda Kingdom—members of the Lukiko, cabinet members and many others. Your love for Buganda Kingdom and commitment to serve is a cut above the rest.

My gratitude to the last four Prime Ministers (ba Katikiro) with whom I have had the opportunity to work: Joseph Mulwanyamuli Ssemwogerere, Dan Muliika, Emmanuel Ssendawula, John Baptist Walusimbi, and Charles Peter Mayiga for your dedication toward the preservation and promotion of our culture, and growth and advancement of Buganda Kingdom. Apollo Makubuya and David Mpanga, thank you for the invaluable counsel through the years.

One's productivity depends a lot on their wellbeing at home. I am grateful to my household staff at Kireka Palace: Jajja Jasi (RIP), Ssenga Juliet Nabwami, Alex Kafero, Joseph Kawoya, Hannington Kamya, Sarah Luyiiga, Khasfa Bakilisa, Godfrey Lubade, George William Mpanga, Jajja Eseza, Josey Nakyejwe, Rose Nakimbugwe, Uma Muyingo, Haji Sendikwanawa (RIP), Julius Mulyanga, Hawa Nasimbwa, Eddy Sempijja, Kaddu Peter, Samuel Buyondo, Juliet Nakuya, Hadija Nakawesi, Davis Kibuuka, Sarah Ndagire, Kunobwa, Tony Ntege, Wilberforce Kavuma, Edward Mawanda, Muzafaru Sendi, Andrew Kibuuka, Moses Kayiwa, Fred Mugumya, Tito Kalibala, Peter Senkayi and many others. Your work ethic, passion, and dedication in providing household services like childcare, cooking, cleaning, laundering, gardening, pet care, maintenance, transportation and security has enhanced my wellbeing and brought such fulfilment to our lives and that of our guests. Without you, I wouldn't have done half of what I have been able to do or achieve. Thank you so very much.

Under the leadership of Cate Bwete, thank you Regina Nabukenya, Susan Nanono, Lillian Musoke, and Lydia Namuswa for being on top of all the Kireka Palace administration—coordinating and supervising your coworkers.

Extra special thanks to all my relatives and friends who accepted my invitation to be interviewed for this book. I didn't realise how much I meant to you. Your contributions have tremendously enriched my story. I'm so glad to have met you.

Maama Faith Luwalira and Nita Babumba for your faith and love for God. You brought me closer to God by standing with me at my lowest point through Bible studies, prayer sessions, and mentoring and guidance. Reverend Abel Meerewooma and Reverend Desmond Serunjogi for being mountains of hope. You continue to play a critical role in my spiritual journey.

To Fiona Magona for your unwavering commitment and wise counsel—guiding me through the legal nuts and bolts which, without you, I couldn't have figured out. And to Lisa Romesburg for facilitating the writing of this book in the most cordial and professional manner that has kept the process moving from the very beginning to the end.

Finally, to Dr Dennis Sempebwa for your intelligence, patience, and resilience. I am grateful to God for always giving me the best. He certainly led me to the right person to write my story. I couldn't have asked for anybody else. Your positive attitude, energy, enthusiasm, and commitment to excellence is inspiring. Thank you for assuring me that the best would be done—and indeed we have sailed through countless interviews with family, friends, well-wishers—people I have met along this remarkable journey, people who have walked with me, loved me, prayed for me, and supported our causes.

Most importantly, to my Lord God who continues to grant me the grace to serve and be salt and light in this troubled world.

*Sylvia Nagginda Luswata*
The Nnaabagereka

# CONTENTS

# PROLOGUE

On August 27, 1999, I became the Nnaabagereka of Buganda. Me, a simple girl had fallen in love with a king and become his wife—the queen in one of Africa's great civilisations, the Buganda Kingdom! I was extremely grateful for the opportunity to serve a special people who had thrived for more than 800 years.

As I basked in the warmth of this indescribable honour, reality quickly set in...my life as an ordinary girl had ceased. I had stepped into a large, undefined role. I assumed colossal responsibilities for the people of Buganda, and along with that, their high expectations. I had to be the Nnaabagereka from the moment I said my vows to marry their Kabaka.

I was a normal girl, but henceforth, no more. You see, our subjects fully expected me to act like royalty. Yes...I had to do and say the right things 100 percent of the time. There was absolutely no room for mistakes. I felt like I was almost set up to fail them, especially since I had no such grooming.

I grappled with the cultural definitions of my role. Who exactly is the Nnaabagereka? What was expected of me? There was no defined role for Nnaabagereka other than vague generalisations such as, 'You are the wife of the Kabaka, and you exist to support him, go to functions with him, bear his children, and be his wife'!

*Not bad*, I thought, *I can handle that!* But was that all?

Thankfully, I quickly found my bearings. After eighteen years in the United States, this was the beginning of a new chapter in my life: an exciting chapter that challenges conventional wisdom on how change can happen in the 21$^{st}$ century. As Nnaabagereka, I was placed close to the apex of a traditional cultural value system in a modern world and, above all, to grow as a leader, while setting the pace for fellow African women leaders.

The title Nnaabagereka is derived from the Luganda word *okugereka* that means 'to prepare and apportion' and 'to serve'. I had two distinct choices: 1) maintain the status quo, be the traditional wife and stay safe; or 2) play an active role in shaping our community and our beloved nation.

I chose to do both.

This is my story.

SECTION
1

# OKWEZUULA
(Self-Discovery)

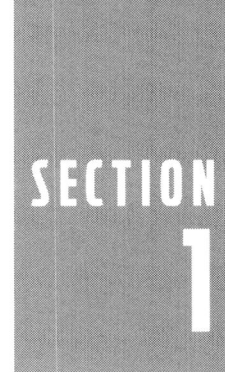

# 'Mazzi Masabe Tegaloga Nyonta'

(Luganda Proverb)

Translation:
*'Water Obtained by Begging
Cannot Quench One's Thirst'*

# chapter 1

# EKIBAYA

## (Crib)

'No...I want my baby! Please don't take my baby away'! yelled Rebecca Nakintu Musoke at the top of her lungs. With that, the adoption agency left.

Life had not turned out the way she had hoped. Mum had come to England to study nursing on a scholarship.

> 'My teacher took a liking for me. He said I would make a great nurse if I got further training. Next thing I know we are applying for a scholarship from the Kabaka Foundation. A few months later, I was on my way to Stratford-upon-Avon School of Nursing in England'.
>
> —*Rebecca Musoke* (Mother)

As fate would dictate, she reconnected with a handsome young man she had met in Uganda, named John Mulumba Luswata, at Northern Polytechnic (presently University of North London). Like her, John was a student on scholarship.

John had taken a liking to Mum. Naturally, his attentions were much too flattering for a young girl living so far away from her home, so she fell for him. The two started hanging out and travelling away on short breaks to the English countryside.

When Mum became pregnant, all hell broke loose. Having a child out of wedlock was scorned upon in that small conservative English town of Shakespeare Village.

'When I found out that I was pregnant, I was terrified out. The Ugandan embassy had standing orders from our government to return unwed pregnant students back to Uganda, so I couldn't let anyone know about it. I was mad at John, mad at me, and mad at everyone! Needless to say, my sponsor was devastated. She moved me into a young mothers' shelter and found a social worker to walk me through the next few months. The shelter was comfortable, but I was extremely isolated. I was the only black girl there'.

—*Rebecca Musoke* (Mother)

Mom was forced out of school for the remaining five months of her pregnancy for fear of what they called 'negative influence' on the other girls. The shelter provided full prenatal care until delivery. Their policy was to immediately place the newborn child into foster care to prevent the young mother from attaching to the baby.

When the time had come, she was admitted to Leamington Spa Hospital. It is on that winter afternoon of November 9, 1962, that I was born to my frightened mother in the small town of Warwickshire, United Kingdom.

# A WHITE DOVE

The nurse placed me in my mother's arms. She was very happy. She said she couldn't get her eyes off of me. Some of the other mothers said that they had never seen a black baby before. Remember this was in the early sixties.

Visitors were walking in and out of our ward. Some stopped by to say hello, but none had come to see Mom. She was afraid and lonely. Aside from her social worker, it seemed as though no one really cared about her or even knew her.

> 'As visiting hours ended on the third day, the ward became deafeningly quiet once again. My eyes started to shut. Suddenly, I was startled by a rattling noise. A white dove flew into the room and stood on my bed, right next to Sylvia. I tried to swoosh it away but couldn't. My wardmates came out to see the gentle bird. "Oh my God…you have a visitor today sent by God"! The bird lingered for what felt like forever, and then flew out the same window'.
>
> —*Rebecca Musoke* (Mother)

My mother never understood the meaning of that visitation, but somehow she knew it was significant. Decades later, she still thinks it was meaningful. Somehow, I do too.

As with other girls, the home insisted upon immediate adoption.

Two days later, Mum's social worker came to discharge her. We were taken back to the shelter where we would stay until a more permanent home was found for me.

'I didn't know how to take care of her. I remember this one evening, Sylvia had been crying for hours. I couldn't console her, so I decided to just lay her next to me. We both drifted off to sleep. Next thing I hear is my panicked nurse. She couldn't find Sylvia. We looked around, but no one knew where my baby was. Out of desperate resignation, I thought to look under the bed, and there she was. Somehow, she had rolled off the bed on to the floor, and under the bed. Thankfully, she was fine'.

—*Rebecca Musoke* (Mother)

They found a foster home, and for four and a half months, a generous English family provided excellent care for me.

'One thing I remember is they had problems combing her black hair. She had a sensitive scalp, so every time they tried, she yowled with pain. They decided to wait for me to do it whenever I visited. Unfortunately, Sylvia started to associate my visits with pain, so she hated my visits. I wished I could take care of her. I wished I could send her to my mother, but she was unwell. She had also just given birth to a newborn, my sister Milly'.

—*Rebecca Musoke* (Mother)

My grandfather, Nelson Sebugwawo, was visiting London on government business. He was eager to see his son's child, but had not been able to. When he asked to see Mum, she had an interesting proposition for him. Since she and John were still in school, she suggested that he, Jajja Nelson, should consider taking me back with him and raise me instead of the British foster care system.

He heartily agreed.

'Given our circumstances, we couldn't take care of her. We looked at adoption but decided instead to send her back to Uganda. My mother and father would take care of her until we were done with school. Giving my daughter away like this was one of the hardest decisions I had to make'.

—*John Luswata* (Father)

Finally, the day had arrived. My grandfather couldn't fly back to London to pick up this five-month-old baby, so a lovely lady, Ursula Sentongo, offered to fly me back with her to Entebbe in Uganda.

'It was a sunny morning when that British Airways flight landed at Entebbe Airport. We'd been waiting for this day for weeks. They told us that the baby would be delivered to us through one of the flight attendants. Dad was caught up with palace business, so he couldn't come. I remember when they handed the crib to mummy. She was beautiful. To me, she wasn't a niece. She was a sibling. She was one of us—a baby sister'.

—*Cate Bamundaga* (Aunt)

On that warm February afternoon of 1963, I was handed to my grandparents to be raised in the safety, ways, and traditions of my people.

'Initially, they told us that we wouldn't see her until she was old enough to travel. But then suddenly, they said she was being brought home. So, we all went to

Nkumba to welcome her. At around 2 p.m., the car arrived with this tiny baby in a crib. She was so cute. We didn't want to leave'.

—*Kolya Ekiriya* (Aunt)

They gave me a nickname *mwana wa mu kibaya* meaning, 'crib baby'.

'I remember feeling the pangs of jealousy. This new baby seemed to take up way too much of my mother's time. I would learn that the baby had to receive a daily shot from our family doctor, Dr Sembeguya in Kawempe. No one told me why, and I didn't really bother asking. But somehow, I just took it upon myself to ensure she never missed her visits. I was convinced she might die if she didn't take her shot or missed her visits. I remember missing my sister's wedding ceremony because we had a doctor's visit that day. Somehow, I figured that Sylvia's wellbeing was far more important. She was my baby sister. In fact, we had named her Sylvia Sebugwawo'.

—*Cate Bamundaga* (Aunt)

## A HAPPY HOME

My grandparents became father and mother to me. I called them Taata and Maama meaning father and mother (in English). They were all I knew and all I had. Their children, who were technically my uncles and aunties, were my big brothers and sisters. I was close in age to the two youngest boys, so we played games and did life together as siblings.

'"You are going to have to skip your playtime, and head straight back here after school so you can help take care of the baby," Mother instructed. Just like that, I became the official nanny. I remember taking her for medical visits to Dr Sembeguya's clinic in Kawempe. She was a very calm baby—not much crying, just sucking her thumb…'

*—Eva Nassejje* (Aunt)

Taata's house was warm and full of life. Built in 1914, he had inherited it from his own father, my great grandfather, Saulo Sebugwawo.

Taata had twenty-eight children: thirteen from his first wife, my grandmother Jajja Catherine Namayaza Sebugwawo (Maama), ten from the second wife, Jajja Robinah Naluwoza Sebugwawo, and five others. Although we didn't all live in the same house, yes…ours was a full house most of the time. 'God has blessed me with a large family', Taata would say, 'and along with it, the ability to provide for them'.

Taata had the biggest heart. There was always plenty of food to eat and milk to drink. We were really blessed with abundance. I still remember the huge evening meals. He and some of the grownups would sit up at the dining table, while we, the kids and Maama, sat on floor mats right next to them. Meals were a communal affair. We all had to eat at the same time and the same food—whatever was cooked for the day is what we all shared, no exceptions. You couldn't be picky with the menu or preparations.

I feel blessed with some of the fondest memories any child could ever wish for. No one made me feel any different from the other kids. Our home was warm and peaceful. Even though we were many at times, I really didn't feel it. As far as I was concerned, the more the merrier. Besides, we had plenty of space outside to play.

> 'I was five years old when we met. She was introduced to me as Uncle John's daughter. Straight away, we bonded. I remember playing kitchen one day. We had made a fire and placed bits of what I thought were coffee beans in the makeshift pan to represent the main meal. Just as we started to eat, a neighbour runs up to us and summarily brings a halt to our pretend dinner. Turns out the coffee beans were goat droppings!'
>
> —*Fred Lutalo* (Cousin)

## THIS IS YOUR DAD

My grandfather (Taata) named me Nagginda a name from his clan, the Musu (Cane Rat) Clan which I am part of and is one of the 52 clans of Buganda. The clan in Buganda represents a group of people who can trace their lineage to a common ancestor, and it is central to the Ganda culture. In the customs of Buganda, lineage is passed down along the same lines and the most important unit in Buganda's culture is the clan. The clan in Buganda forms a large extended family. Members of the same clan regard each other as brothers and sisters regardless of how far they are in terms of actual blood ties.

I remember first seeing my father when he came to Nkumba soon after he returned from the United Kingdom (UK).

They told me he was my real father. I disliked the idea of it all. See, all along I knew that my grandfather was my father. I had called him 'Taata'. So now I suddenly had a 'real father'? I did not like to see him, so I would hide from him whenever he came to Nkumba to visit us. My grandparents made several attempts to take me over to his house to stay, but I wouldn't have it.

I remember when he once came to visit me at Gayaza High School and I told my friends that he was my uncle. They all knew who my Taata was. At that time, I carried his last name Sebugwawo as my own family name.

> 'It was time to get back into my daughter's life, who at the time was still living in Nkumba with my parents. I remember going to the farm to see her. Even though I was her father, she really didn't know me. Sadly, we were strangers. As far as she was concerned, her real father was my father'.
>
> —*John Luswata* (Father)

In spite of the rejection, my father was always happy, smiling, and making jokes. They explained to me how he had been studying in London and he was now back home, working for the Ministry of Health as an electrical technician. Of course, none of it made any sense to me. Deep down, I feared that this rather young-looking new father would take me away from my grandparents and the safety of the only home I knew.

*What? No way. . .I already have my Taata and my Maama!* I thought to myself. As with many things in my culture, no one cared to explain the shocking encounter to me. I couldn't understand how someone could just come and claim to be my dad. I was confused.

I was angry and basically rejected him. To me, he was a spoiler, a disrupter. I didn't want to have anything to do with him.

But I couldn't change this terrible arrangement. I remember my first visit with him. Maama took me to his house but didn't tell me that she would leave me there with this stranger they said was my father. When we arrived, I thought, *I don't have to warm up to him. This will be over soon.* Again, no one explained what was really happening. I hadn't noticed the extra bag that Maama had with clothes in it.

Suddenly, she gets up to leave. Then it dawns on me. She was leaving me there. I panicked and lost it! I screamed at the top of my lungs and took off chasing that white Volkswagen (Beetle). 'Don't leave me here! Please don't leave me here'! I pleaded. They never turned back. They left me there. And for hours I was decidedly disconsolate. I just couldn't reconcile the harsh abandonment. *How could Maama do this to me?*

> 'After his return back to Uganda, John really wanted to get back into his daughter's life. He genuinely wanted to spend time with her. Well, that didn't go over well at all. She didn't know him, so she absolutely hated the whole arrangement. I remember dropping her off after school one afternoon. She was livid. She chased the car all the way down the driveway. Dad couldn't take it. He stopped the car, picked her up, and we drove back to Nkumba'.
>
> —*Cate Bamundaga* (Aunt)

Unfortunately for me, this visit would not be the last. Taata and Maama started to schedule periodic outings for me with Dad. They honestly wanted to do right by the both of us. They wanted us to build a relationship, but I wouldn't have it. For a long time, I couldn't call him daddy.

I dreaded the visits—at first in New Mulago and later Old Mulago staff quarters where my dad stayed. For hours, I'd be left alone with the house help because he had to go to work. I made friends with the kids next door, which was always a great consolation. Sometimes, Dad had to ask Maama to come get me because I was miserable. Often, I just wanted to go back to my real home in Nkumba.

## THIS IS YOUR MUM

The re-entry of my father into my life created questions I never had.

*If Taata is not my real father, then what about Maama?*

Great perplexity was once again my unwelcome companion.

Details were scanty. 'Your mom lives in Europe. Isn't it wonderful to have a mother in England'? they mused. I was unimpressed. *So I have a mother out there? Will I ever meet her?* I was confused.

The first time I saw my mother was on a sunny afternoon in 1972 when she came to Nkumba. My granny asked me to come to the living room and greet the guests. I had been told earlier on that day that my mother from America was coming to see me. By then, I had learnt that she had moved from the

UK to the United States (US). But before I appeared to greet the guests, I had to be made presentable since I had been playing and was smudged with dirt. They cleaned me up, gave me a change of clothes, and applied ample Vaseline on my body that my face was literally shining.

I walked in from behind the seat where my Maama's chair was, which was also near the entrance from the back of the house where I had been playing. I stood motionless but smiling next to my Maama. There were several people in the living room. They all looked at me curiously, clearly anticipating my reaction. My eyes wondered around the room, and right in front of me was a lady with a foreign look, smiling broadly in my direction. The room was quiet.

Suddenly, I heard someone ask, *'Omutegede'*? meaning, 'Do you recognise her'? Then the foreign-looking lady responded, *'Mutegedde,'* meaning, 'Yes I have.' All eyes were on me: clearly, they anticipated a particular response from me. To break the anxiety in the room, my Maama prompted me to go ahead and greet the lady—my mother—which I did. It was no different from greeting any other guest on any other day in my Taata's living room.

Important as I am sure it was, that moment didn't resonate with me as I am certain it should have. As I was contemplating a response, the adults broke out into another long conversation.

The whole thing was awkward to me. Yes, I had met my 'real mother'. And again, just like with my father, I could not connect with her. Emotionally, she was another stranger who somewhat threatened my sense of balance and safety.

'I witnessed her journey as she came to terms with her heritage and identity. Here is a young girl who had been raised by her grandparents, being re-introduced to her birthparents after having been separated from them since birth, and on top of all that, being expected to bond with them. It was understandably difficult'.

—*Eva Nassejje* (Aunt)

My mother returned a few days later, this time to take me to spend some time with her at my maternal grandparents in Nazigo Kyagwe village. On our way there, we stopped in Nakasero, a suburb in Kampala City, for a few days to visit an uncle who was a doctor. We took many second-hand household items which my mum had purchased from departing Asians who had been abruptly expelled from the country by the then-infamous president Idi Amin Dada.

The Indian community had been the main custodians of the country's business and industrial prosperity. They had been given ninety days to leave the country and everything they called home. Suddenly, desperate Indian families were eager to unload merchandise and household items for next to nothing. That single legislation would later devastate the country's economy.

Well, like anyone who could, my mother had purchased some of these items for her parents: a new living room set, dining tables, chairs, beds, and many more other items. My grandparents and the entire family were so delighted to receive the items.

My maternal grandparents' house in Nazigo Kyaggwe was very different from the home I grew up in at Nkumba. It was much smaller, and it stood close to the main road. It had no electricity, so at night we used lanterns.

My mother's father, Mr George Musoke, was a small-time coffee grower and a shopkeeper. His shop, which was part of the house, was also a centre for other coffee growers. They would bring their coffee produce to get weighed and sold to buyers who would then take the beans for processing. The area was a busy village shopping centre.

Although clearly this side of my family wasn't as well-off as my father's side, it was a very happy home. My mother's sisters and brothers were friendly and welcoming. My grandfather and mother were delighted to have me over. I enjoyed myself as I played and bonded with them.

The village was bustling with both small and large-scale farming. It had huge banana, sugar, and coffee plantations. The area was vibrant with business as big trucks came in and out to take the produce to the markets.

I enjoyed my stay as I met more relatives and made new friends. I remember a girl named Harriet Mwenyango who was my playmate. My uncle Lubowa made a fashion model out of me when he would get me dressed up, take me outside his house, which was next to grannie's house, to take pictures of me. There was a prayer service and a big feast organised for my mother.

I must have spent a couple of weeks at Nazigo. Mum wasn't there with me while I was there. She had left for the city a few days after we arrived; she came back and stayed for a couple of nights before she took me back to my grandparents in Nkumba.

While at Nazigo, my Maama was concerned about my poor eating conditions, and was upset that Mum had left me there for so many days.

Several days later she returned to New York. It would be ten years before I saw her again.

We did stay in touch via post mail and on phone from time to time. She would send me clothes, shoes, purses, and other items through her cousin, Uncle Keffa Kyambade, who used to work at Uganda Television (UTV). He lived in the station staff quarters in a one-room house where I would pick up my things whenever I was invited. At the time, getting clothes from America was a very big thing! I felt really special. I was proud of having my mother in America. I remember talking about her to my friends and anyone whoever cared to listen.

# chapter 2

# EMISINGI
## (Foundations)

Taata owned hundreds of square miles of land all around *Nkumba* and indeed much of Entebbe District and other vast areas within Buganda Kingdom. In a culture that considers landownership the surest measure of real wealth, this made him an extra-ordinarily rich man. Around the village, he was called *Omutaka* (or Chief) Sebugwawo, as indeed he served at the pleasure of the king of Buganda.

> 'When I became our father's heir after his death, I also took over his parish as chief. In my culture then, the heir also assumed his father's position'.
> —The Late Nelson Sebugwawo (Grandfather)

My earliest memories were at my paternal grandparents' house in Nkumba. I must have been 4 years old. I remember playing at the back of the house by a big ground water tank, nestled under a big tree which we often climbed.

Adjacent to the kitchen was Jajja Anna Nabwami's room. She was our elderly grandmother, light skinned, grey haired, and of short stature with a bent posture. I must have been 6 years old when she passed on. I was jokingly told I would be her heir, something that frightened me so much that I literally ran away from the burial grounds. She was the first close relative I knew to have died.

One other elder person who stood out was Bijiji, one of Taata's attendants from Burundi who had lived with the family for many years and had become a household name in the entire village. He was a scary man, a drunkard who would come home drunk almost every night—shouting out my grandfather's name to the rest of the village, 'Sebugwawo Bayitawo'!

## FARM LIFE

Farther down from the main house were farm paddocks with vast herds of cattle. My grandfather was a big dairy farmer. In fact, he literally named his cows after his children and grandchildren. And yes, one of the cows was named Nagginda, after me.

Taata would get up to supervise the first milking of cows at around 4 a.m. Even though he had hired a farm manager and many other workers, he was very much hands-on. He often said that being around his cows brought him peace and serenity.

At 6 a.m., the cows would be taken out to graze away from the main house, which along with the farm paddocks and milking stalls, stood on about 30 acres of land. Around mid-afternoon, they were taken to a place called a 'dip' to get disinfected before heading back to the food and water stalls for their second milking.

It was such fun watching the cows being milked. The herdsmen (or *balalo*, as we used to call them), would squat beside the cows as they whistled and sang special songs for them. They would wiggle their tails as though to express their appreciation.

The balalo knew me well, often indulging my curiosity and showing me how to milk the cows. It was an exciting feeling touching the cow's udder and pulling their teats downward for milk. And as you would expect, my fingers were too small, too slow and soon enough, my trainer quickly ended my lesson.

I befriended the balalos' families. I remember there was one particular mulalo's wife who really became fond of me. I would go into their little house not far from the main house and visit with her—she would often give me some food to eat that my grandmother didn't approve of.

Then there were trips to the vet, our veterinary doctor. I remember Fred and I sneaking in the back of the truck, something that earned us some scolding from Maama. Beyond treating cows, the vet's place also served as a processing and packaging depot for milk. The huge jugs were transported to the market for sale. Our farm supplied most of Entebbe and neighbouring towns.

The main house had three bedrooms, and all the children slept in one room no matter how many—we had bunk beds.

There was always enough food to eat, even for those who showed up unannounced. We would have breakfast at 10 a.m., lunch at 4 p.m., afternoon tea at 8 p.m. and dinner at around 11 p.m., sometimes as late as midnight. One guest we always looked forward to having was our great grandmother from Manyangwa—Jajja Sarah Namyenya. She had so many funny stories that kept us in stiches and there was never a dull moment with her around. For fear of catching a cold she always carried her plate and cup.

## HOMESTEADS

Taata had two wives, both of whom occasionally (separately or together) accompanied him to official functions. Something I thought was normal until much later when I learnt more about international norms. Two wives meant two homes—the farmhouse where Maama lived being the principal residence. Taata took turns spending a week at one home and the following week at another.

Taata was strict and feared. The nights that he spent away from the farmhouse were such a pleasure for us children. We would freely make noise in the house and would also be able to sit in front of the black and white TV and watch to our hearts' content, something that we would never do when he was home.

While this was enjoyable to us, I later realised that Maama would have much preferred to have her husband spend all the nights with her.

As the story goes, Maama got married to Taata in her early teens. Several years later with 6 children between them, one day Taata brings home a girl who is almost as young as his firstborn to be his second wife. The young girl was Robinah Naluwaga from Kooki. These were very difficult times for my grandmother Catherine. My daddy held on to those painful childhood memories—his mother's pain and suffering—to the day he died at the age of 81. The violation and mental abuse that his mother experienced shaped my father's own perspective on marriage— promising never to marry more than one wife. In fact, at my sister Barbara's wedding, during his speech he asked the groom, his future son-in-law, to 'never add another woman to my daughter'.

Understandably, as a child, I was oblivious to the emotional roller coaster that existed between my two grandmothers and their husband. As far as we knew, Taata was running two families and two wives. There was mama *we'Nkumba* (meaning the Maama at Nkumba, our farmhouse) and mama *wo'kuluguudo* (or Mama residing in the house by the main road).

Running two families must have been strenuous for Grandpa. In hindsight, I'd say it was quite a mind-boggling juggle. He was generally quiet especially when it came to answering his wives' consistent squabbling about the various issues in the homes. He would listen most of the time and give one-word answers. I remember eavesdropping outside their bedroom door. We could hear Maama often speaking her mind, expressing her disappointments, and making her demands. For most of the conversation, Taata would be quiet, no doubt feeling dejected. He'd have similar conversations at Kulugudo with his other wife, Mama Robinah.

'Although she was born in the UK, Nagginda was raised by her grandparents at Nkumba. The Sebugwawo home was run as a traditional high-class Kiganda home, where the patriarch grandfather was treated as a king. Grown men had to prostrate and women had to kneel, when talking to him. Growing up in this home, Nagginda was taught proper Luganda and high class Kiganda behaviour that is controlled, calm, polite and dignified. Consequently, she has a very strong sense of decorum'.

—Jean Sembeguya Matovu (Friend)

## OBLIVIOUS

Taata was a fun person. He liked exposing us to different forms of entertainment and learning. He would take us to the zoo, game parks, to plays and music shows, and the children's circus. He would take the boys to see football games and boxing matches. He would also take us to traditional events, like when I was about 9 years old in 1971. It was one of the events that was organised for then Prince Ronald Mutebi upon his return home from the UK for the official burial of his father, the late Ssekabaka Mutesa II.

I remember the venue, a place called Kakeeka, near the golf course in Entebbe. There was a church nearby. I remember the big crowd and the jubilation when we saw the Crown Prince. His father, Kabaka Mutesa, had passed away only two years before. Memories of the fallen king and the abolished Kingdom were still very fresh.

Seeing the prince gave hope to many that maybe someday, the Buganda Kingdom could be restored. As the young prince sat on the raised platform in front of the crowd, people were ecstatic. The sound of kiganda music and drums permeated Entebbe town as orators and speakers praised and encouraged the young prince.

I don't remember what was said or much else about the auspicious occasion. At 9 years of age, I was one of those kids who didn't make much of jubilations or the musings of adulthood. None of my age-mates really understood the fuss at the time. I still remember the grownups being so excited. My other relatives and I sneaked out of the main grounds to play our own games, running around and drinking soda from bottles. Oh and we had no openers. We used teeth, and guess who was designated bottle opener? Yours truly! I distinctly remember running around with a bottle of Fanta in my hands and stopping to stare at the prince seated in front of the crowd, before taking off to return to play. Little did I know that twenty-eight years later, he'd be my husband.

## MAAMA (My Paternal Grandmother)

Maama (grandmother) has been the most influential person in my life. At 5 months old, she welcomed me with open arms and did not even once ever make me feel less-than, or second tier.

I could never forget her lessons. She taught me etiquette and manners, the importance of discretion, the value of character and integrity, the art of cooking, the usefulness of service to others, respect for elders and my older siblings and aunties, and so much more.

> 'Sylvia was very playful, yet calm. She was a vigourous advocate for fairness. You never heard any stories of her playing hooky with the boys on the farm. She was a homebody who loved the company of her grandparents and liked to help out around the house. She cooked, cleaned, ironed, sewed, and did countless chores efficiently. One thing is for sure…that girl was raised right. In fact, I found it rather humourous when the media wondered if she knew how to work with her hands'.
> —Eva Nassejje (Aunt)

Maama taught me how to carry myself as a young lady. Since most of the women in the house were much older than me, I gravitated towards the boys. Consequently, I often thought I could get into whatever they did. I was a tough girl. I milked cows and climbed *miyembe* (mangos) and *mapapaali* (paw paw) trees. I can still remember Maama's admonishments, '*Abakyala tebakola'ebyo*' meaning, 'Women don't do things like that'! She was always concerned about games like hide-and-seek. Without saying so, she was fearlessly protective of my chastity. Truth be told, she didn't care for my tough-girl image. She preferred the good old fashioned traditional femininity.

Maama was a consummate disciplinarian, never mincing words especially when she communicated boundaries. With that also came the punishments. If you crossed a line, you could expect decisive consequences, even if they didn't come immediately. One thing we all dreaded was her long memory. If the long lecture didn't work, then she would let her *muzingoonyo* do the talking. A *muzingoonyo* is a cutout from the stem of a banana tree. It was the preferred tool for spanking because it had a soft outer shell which didn't bruise like a wooden switch or stick does.

'Her grandmother Kasalina was fond of her. She was rather stern and relentless in keeping her in line. For example, no one was allowed to go to bed without joining the family for nightly prayers. Sylvia was often chosen to read Bible verses'.

—Ann-Loi Nangendo Fulu (Aunt)

One day, my auntie Robinah Namusoke paid us a surprise visit. She had brought with her a rather cute young girl. As she got up to leave, she breaks the news to us: 'It's time for me to go, but I am leaving her here'! I will never forget the traumatic separation. Cate Nabankema was pulling on her mother's dressing and desperately begging not to be left behind.

'My mother dropped me off in Nkumba completely unannounced and of course against my will. I was only 4 years old. So, you can imagine that I was upset, alone, and confused. Sylvia immediately picked me up, comforted me and walked me around for hours. Before long, her warm love and company made me forget about my misery. We'd play for hours and hours, and really bonded. And then there were those dreaded countless chores. Most notably, Jajja's bedroom. Yes, we were responsible for its upkeep. But like every chore, we sometimes slacked off. I still remember hearing Jajja yelling our names: "Siliviya…Nabankema…". I knew there was trouble. Without warning, she would shut the door, pull out her switch…and yes, she'd put us straight. No misdeed went unpunished, even if she had to wait till bedtime'.

—Cate Nabankema Bwete (Cousin)

My cousin, Fred Lutalo, and I were close in age, so we bickered and fought a lot. I didn't care that he was a boy, and that he was stronger than me. I held my own. I still remember the one time when we got into it on the back stairway. He pushed my buttons, or perhaps I should say we pushed each other's buttons, and the next thing I knew we were wrestling on the ground in a bitter fist fight. We both knew we'd get into big trouble if Maama found out—especially me because decent girls don't fist-fight, right? So, no one ever mentioned it again, until now! Truth be told, we didn't want to experience her *muzingoonyo*.

Maama was very protective of all her children and grand-children. She always saw the good in all of us. She was my safety net, never throwing me under the bus, even when I was at fault. Sometimes, she served as a buffer between me and Taata.

'As a teenager Sylvia had a passion for James Hadley Chase novels. In an era where we had a landline phone that had to be connected through the post office and no video games, she spent most of her evenings reading. Surprisingly, Grandma thought Sylvia was reading school textbooks. She would tell us to not to bother Sylvia because she was "busy studying", unlike the rest of us who were loitering around'.

—Ann-Loi Nangendo Fulu (Aunt)

Without Maama's influence, I would not be the woman, mother, friend, wife or leader I am today. Much as I would have desired to grow up in a conventional home with my birth mother, father, and siblings, I am so thankful to God for choosing to add me to the Sebugwawo household.

'She was always a very good girl. My parents brought her up very well. They loved her so very much that it looked as if they favoured her more than us. They in fact gave her more than they gave us. Clearly, Sylvia was a favourite'.

—Sarah Kamya (Aunt)

I never wanted to lose Maama and Taata. They were God's precious gifts to me. Their unconditional love made me feel safe. Whenever Maama travelled away, I was worried. I would be watching the front gate, afraid that she wasn't coming back home. I was gripped with a palpable fear of separation.

Did my childhood separation from my mum exacerbate those emotions, even though I wasn't really mentally aware of it? Perhaps. At any rate, we know that in our kids' minds, everything is huge! A day apart feels like a week. As a mother, I often wondered about my own daughters, Ssanga, Jade and Jasmine. Did they struggle, as I did, with the fear of me not returning home one day?

## TAATA (My Paternal Grandfather)

Aside from crop farming, Taata was a successful livestock farmer. 'Soon after school, I began practicing agriculture. I have raised cattle, chicken, ducks, turkeys, goats, and pigs', he used to proudly say.

I remember how little I felt standing next to the large paddocks which housed the hundreds of cows. We used to supply milk to the whole district of Entebbe.

One of my early memories was the time when Fred and I sneaked into the truck that took milk to the vet. It wasn't until we got to the main road that they noticed their unwelcome passengers. Needless to say, we received a stern 'admonition' that night. We never attempted to do that again.

Taata raised me the old fashioned, no-nonsense way.

'Long time ago, my neighbour's children were considered my own. I would discipline them if I saw them go astray and support them if and when they needed it'.
    —The Late Nelson Sebugwawo (Grandfather)

Before the abolition of tribal monarchies, Taata had served at the pleasure of His Majesty King Mutesa II as the *Omuwanika* (or Treasurer). He lived to be 103 years old. Interestingly, I sit in the exact same office in Bulange, Mengo, where he sat five decades ago. I still remember the stunned look on his face when he first came to visit me here in 2000, about a year after I was married, 'This used to be my office', he exclaimed.

While home, when the younger boys my age were away, I learnt to play alone since all the other females in the house were older than me. I learnt how to play house, make dresses for my dolls, and from time to time, seek out the workers' kids to play with them. I would occupy myself for hours.

I also learnt to make friends with the other girls in the village. We would play hide and seek, and *kasonko*, a local game akin to hop and skip (hopscotch). The large compound made for some of the most elaborate playtimes a kid could ever dream of.

> 'One Christmas eve, I decided we should wait up to see the birth of baby Jesus. I had read that Jesus Christ was born in a manger. Well, to me, the kraals in the back of the house looked just like the pictures of the Bethlehem manger. For hours, we literally sat there with Sylvia and waited for the Holy Child to be born, but He never showed up. We were very disappointed'.
> –Fred Lutalo (Cousin)

Life with my uncles was a bit different. We were closer in age, especially with Eddie Serukeberwa, Alon Lumala and Nelson Kiraga. I'd hang out with them for hours. We'd talk fast cars and all kinds of things boys like to talk about. Again, Maama wasn't amused. I'd hear her scream: *'Siliviya, vayo mubalenzi'!* meaning, 'Sylvia, stay away from the boys'!

While Eddie and Lumala went to boarding schools, Nelson and I went to the same day school, Lake Victoria. So he and I were very close. While in secondary school, Nelson tragically contracted an illness that disrupted his education. This was a great blow to the family. I was devastated to see my friend go through a very difficult time at such an early age.

One thing I remember vividly was the large number of people around the house.

In our Buganda culture, it was customary to expect visiting relatives to show up without notice or invitation. Sometimes, they'd even sleep over for several days. The same was the case with friends. They were always welcome to sleep over.

> 'Ours was a large family, but the farm was definitely the place to be. I don't remember a time that Jajja wasn't building something. There was always plenty of sand and mud for brickmaking, which gave us kids lots of opportunities for creativity. We would make mud-houses, mud-kraals, mud-shades and all kinds of structures. We played pretend-brides and grooms in the massive yard. With water in abundance, we also enjoyed water games and played tag in the front section of the property'.
>
> —Robinah Nakamate Kyazze (Aunt)

My biological father John Mulumba Luswata would meet and marry another lady, Edith Kyeyune. They would have two sons Nelson Kikubira and John Mulumba Jr., and two daughters, Barbara and Juliet. There is also mama Edith's son, Patrick Nsubuga whom she had prior to meeting my dad.

On the other side of the world in the USA, my biological mother would also find love and settle down with a Ghanaian gentleman named Maxwell Codjoe. They had two children: Monique and Reuben.

> 'In our P7 classroom, Sylvia's desk was positioned behind mine. We became pretty close as I had a friend to giggle with in between lessons. I became privy to the warm letters she'd receive from her mother, who lived abroad. I also got to know her dad, whose devotion to his eldest child was most touching. Sylvia would speak

very warmly about her family, with Nelson being a particular favourite. I came to love her subtle humour, which often erupted into her infectious belly laugh'.

—Edi Kamya Mpanga (Friend)

Interestingly, these remarriages didn't affect me much at all. I guess I was still somewhat emotionally disconnected from both of my real parents. To me, they were just a distant story.

## A LOVELY LIFE

They say that every village has a drunkard. Well, ours was a sluggard named *Nkoolo*. He lived in a little shack a little distance from us. He wasn't just a hopeless drunk, but a loud one. We could literally hear him hollering blocks away. He and Bijiji got along well especially during their drinking stupors.

Every kid feared him. I was petrified! I remember the grownups threatening, *'Bwoba nga towulira njakutwaala ewa Nkoolo'*. Meaning, 'Hey, if you don't behave, I will take you to Nkoolo'.

We didn't have access to much television to entertain us, except for Saturdays. Taata had a black and white TV set in his living room. Once in a while, we would watch popular American classics like *Bonanza, The Lucy Show, The Beverly Hillbillies, Batman,* and *Scooby Doo*. We would also watch the local drama called *Nebuba nkya Nebuba ngulo* in the evenings especially when Taata was in his other home in Kulugudo. When he was away, we played games and watched television well beyond our normal bedtime. That is when we had some of the loudest and funniest nights.

'Her grandfather was the best man at my parents' wedding. Her grandmother was my godmother. We were playmates whenever our families visited in Nkumba. I remember the Sunday lunches, the games... It was like a kids' paradise. I remember walking in her aunt Cate's wedding: the fittings, the dresses—the thrill! We were just 5 years old'.

—Dr Veronica Nakibule Kalema (Friend)

Life hadn't turned out so badly after all.

Bijiji had nicknames for everyone. He liked to call me *Muk'embuga Nakindaazi,* which loosely means 'the chief's wife'. I remember my nickname because of how it made me feel. I didn't like it. In my young mind, being called chief's wife was awkward, even shameful. It also attracted mockery from the other kids—they would laugh at me.

'Old man Bijiji, who was mostly alone and aloof, never missed an opportunity to call out Sylvia whenever he saw her: *"Gwe Mukembuga Nakindazi"*, meaning "Hey you king or chief's wife and donut..." If Bijiji were alive today, he would say, "I told you so. I knew all along she'd be here! Yes...I believe Sylvia was chosen by God"'!

—Ann-Loi Nangendo Fulu (Aunt)

As I think about this, I am reminded of a Kenyan man, Professor Abukuse Mbirika, I met in the early 1990s in New York. He had developed an affinity for Buganda from the book Empisa Za Baganda, which articulated behaviour norms of our tribe, the Baganda. It was given to him on his first trip to Uganda in the 1950s. We would develop a friendship, but every time he saw me, he insisted on calling me *'Omumbejja'* or 'Princess'. Just like with Bijiji, I didn't like being called princess, so I kept reminding him that I am not a princess. Well, when I spoke to him later after I became queen, he reminded me, 'See, I knew you were royalty'. In hindsight, both these men were unwittingly insightful granted, even somewhat prophetic. God indeed had a much bigger plan for my life.

Taata loved life. He would take us on outings—zoos, landmarks, memorials, boxing matches, swimming and so on. One day he packed the whole lot of us—kids, grandkids, aunties—into a customised Land Rover truck and took us to see the animals in Para National Park in Northeastern Uganda.

One evening at about 6 p.m., we headed out for a game drive. We approached an elephant herd that was standing in the middle of the road. They wouldn't move, so the driver did what experienced game rangers never ever do—he honked at the elephants. One of the mighty beasts got rattled, so it started charging at the truck. We had heard stories of elephants effortlessly toppling vehicles, so we thought we were going to die.

In the middle of the pandemonium, Auntie Gladys and I jumped out of the truck and sprinted for the bushes, not thinking about the other wildlife back there. We were frantic as we tracked over the rough road along the wild grassland. At the desperate beckoning of everyone else in the truck, we turned back. The ranger signaled a truce which turned the mighty elephant away.

# chapter 3

# EBYENGIGIRIZA
## (Education)

Not far from our home in Nkumba, there was a little make-shift preschool we called *'Akasomero ka Mwami Ssagala'*, which means, 'Mr Ssagala's little school', that introduced me to early education. I still remember the fascinating inscriptions on the blackboard. It was the alphabet in Luganda. We would shout them out: 'A... Ba... Cha... Da...'

It was later decided that I should be enroled into a formal pre-school at 'Auntie Clare's' in Mengo. Ms Clare was an English woman who ran a top-notch kindergarten that mostly privileged kids attended. It was exciting.

I don't remember much about my time there, except for the songs we used to sing, my plastic water bottle and my basket school bag. I also remember having to move in with my uncle and aunt, Dan and Joyce Sebugwawo, since they lived within walking distance from Auntie Clare's. The drive to and from Nkumba would have been too long.

As I turned six, it was time to get me into primary school.

'John suggested that Sylvia be enroled into a boarding primary school. They chose Ndejje Girls' School, seeing that my cousin Gladys was headmistress there. Unfortunately, that didn't work out. The following year, she was transferred to Lake Victoria Primary School, where some of my sisters were studying'.
—Cate Bamundaga (Aunt)

I don't remember much about my short time in Ndejje Girl's School, except for the exciting school concerts, learning how to sew, making *emikeeka* (mats) and *ebibbo* (calabashes). I also remember playing with a friend Harriet. However, moving me out of Ndejje so quickly meant that I lost a year of school.

## LAKE VIC

Shortly thereafter, it was decided that I should continue my education in a completely new school, a day school called Lake Victoria Primary School in Entebbe. This meant that I had to move back to Nkumba. I was thrilled, especially since I knew that I'd have company there. Besides my aunts Gladys, Joyce and Robinah, and Uncle Nelson—all children of my grandfather, Taata Sebugwawo—there were also a few kids around the village who attended Lake Victoria School, commonly known as Lake Vic.

The school had two sections: lower school (primary one to three) for students aged 6 to 9, and upper school (primary four to seven) for students aged 10 to 12. Fred and I were in lower school, while Gladys and others were in the upper school.

The transfer to Lake Vic created a glitch in my academic journey. Since I hadn't completed a full year of school at Ndejje, my new school decided to hold me back and make me do primary one over again. Not sure why, but it could have been because of my lack of proficiency in English. Lake Vic had natural-born English teachers who taught us the English language.

Taata had assigned my aunt Gladys, also an older school-mate, to accompany me on my first day at Lake Vic. We sat on one side of the room, with our parents and guardians on the other side, watching us go through our first-day drills. After the exercises, the teacher instructed, 'Now get back to your parents, ok'? I distinctly remember the perplexity, *Wait, but I have no parents to go to.* Then I quickly remembered my proxy, my aunt.

> 'We bunked together in the same room. We'd rise early to a big breakfast—eggs, bread, porridge, with lots of milk. Sylvia loved custard. We'd then jump into one the cars to head out to Lake Vic. Initially, the school had been built for senior government officials during colonial days. In fact, this was the first European school in the country'.
>
> –Fred Lutalo (Cousin)

I don't remember being too bothered by my hold-back in primary one. I was just grateful to be out of boarding school and back home.

Mr J.M. Yates, the headmaster, ran a pretty tight ship. His staff, which was mostly English, were a cut above the rest. Once there, I jumped right in. I engaged in competitive sports like high jump, long jump, and track. I loved winning for my team—the blue team. I was also somewhat of a tom boy, with my antics like the designated 'soda bottle-opener', which I was sternly told that girls didn't do. Too boyish, they'd say.

My friends at Lake Vic were Norah Rwakihembo, Sheila Baingana, Neeta Nabanjja and Pamela Kassami. Neeta, Norah and Pamela were related and lived together in the Rwakihembo household. I would often go over to play after school. Mrs Rwakihembo was an amazing mother. She'd prepare food for us and made me feel at home, like we belonged. We would read books, play house, and make dresses for our dolls. Such memorable times. Sheila was extremely bright, always on top of our class in all subjects. I understand she became a medical doctor, just like her father.

'Sylvia and I met in primary one at Lake Vic. Most of my siblings had a friend in the Sebugwawo family. My brother Bernard was friends with Nelson, Diane with Robinah, Hilda and Gladys, Margaret and Solome, then me, and my two cousins Pamela and Neeta were friends with Sylvia. Our home was conveniently located opposite the school, so our friends visited frequently. We played hide-and-seek, jumped rope, and French skipping using elastic bands tied to the back of chairs or wrapped around two players—we had lots of fun! With very little television time and no internet of course, we would spend most of the time interacting with family and friends. We also loved to read books by Enid Blyton and Agatha Christie'.

—Norah Rwakihembo (Friend)

One day I decided to audition for the annual Christmas play. I was not a prolific singer, but I was assertive. I just sung the loudest, plus I knew all the songs. I was determined to get in, and I did. Well, I made the coveted school choir. After that, I started to believe that I was a really good singer, only to realise later on that I really wasn't.

I remember the Christmas play. We were all dressed up in stunning white dresses—our angel costumes we called them. Our pianist was a smart, light-skinned, charming boy named Richard Ruhweza. Some of the girls thought he was cute. Yeah, okay I thought so too. One thing I knew for sure was that Richard was indeed a genius on the piano.

'Sylvia and I had a blast. I remember acting in a Beauty and the Beast play. We loved potato and sack races. Boy was she a good runner! I remember her being really polite, respectful and very friendly. Both my mother and I thought the world of her'.

—Norah Rwakihembo (Friend)

At Lake Vic, I learnt science, English and math. I was also introduced to reading. I loved reading, which allowed me to excel in English. We exchanged novels and comic books between us. I remember this one girl, Irene Ovonji. She was such an avid reader. I never saw Irene without a book. And I'd often see her walking and reading at the same time, something which a lot of us did. We all loved to read!

'Sylvia was a class ahead of me. She did sports, especially netball and running. People everywhere seemed to like her. Even back at home, she was a favourite. I remember crying my eyes out one day because Grandma had bought her bigger bell bottoms than me. They were the rage those days. And generally, the bigger the better, right? Sylvia enjoyed lots of favour with everyone'.

—Fred Lutalo (Cousin)

## GAYAZA PRIMARY SCHOOL

'*Kati ogenda Gayaza,*' announced Taata, which means, 'Well, now you will be going to Gayaza'.

With those chilling words, my world would once again be turned upside down, and consequently, the trajectory of my life would forever be impacted. I had just completed primary four at Lake Victoria School.

No one explained why I was being transferred. And no one cared to respond to my quizzical stares. See, unlike parents in the West, our African guardians don't bother to explain, much less debate or defend their decisions with their kids. Besides, this didn't seem like a decision I was allowed to debate. Like a 'good' African daughter, I needed to maintain my unshakable belief that they knew what was best for me. And so the following term, I was enroled in Gayaza Primary School.

The school was initially established by the British in 1905 with the purpose of preparing young girls, especially daughters of chiefs, for adulthood. It would become one of the top primary schools in the country, and arguably one of the best performing girls' schools in that part of Africa.

'It is January 1974. We were back at boarding school—Gayaza Junior—to start the new school year. We just got promoted to primary five, having grown up together since primary one. Each year we had newcomers join our close-knit, homogeneous family. This year was interesting. We not only had eight new girls, but they were also rather different from us. They had come from posh day schools where English was the language of the playground. Rita Sebalu, Juliet Mukankusi, Rena Kyewalabye from Norman Godinho, and Peninah Byenkya from Nairobi, and Jennifer Wannyana from Kitante. Then there were the three girls from Lake Vic: Norah, Pamela and Sylvia. They hung out together, Sylvia walking taller than the other two. Coming from a western tribe, Nora and Pamela both struggled with Luganda, which we spoke in the classroom, dining room, playground and dormitory. So these three chose to chat and reminisce in English. We became their captive audience as we listened to their fantastical tales. We'd hear about the flamboyant Miss Oluoch, who I imagine looked like a Hollywood actress. I vividly remember Sylvia mimicking her delicately curled lips and pointed index finger'.

–Edi Kamya Mpanga (Friend)

Although I had been to a boarding school before, this was way more intimidating. New students had to carry two suitcases; one for supplies or what we called 'grub', and another for clothes—the best we had. I was pleasantly surprised to see Norah and Pamela, my old friends from Lake Vic.

> 'Sylvia was brilliant, extremely charming and calm. We made new friends, studied together, laughed, cried, and confided in each other—true friendship it was'!
> —Norah Rwakihembo (Friend)

The first day of school was exciting, but also very intimidating. The school had a culture I needed to get used to—fast. I was joining rather late, in primary five, so most of my classmates were veterans. The well-to-do kids paraded their 'grub' and Saturday was a non-uniform day and so kids would show off their outfits. One term I returned from home with a blouse that had been handmade by my Auntie Betty Sebugwawo. It was made out of a yellow cotton fabric left over from another outfit. I thought it was beautiful, but to my dismay when I wore it the kids laughed at me so hard. I was so hurt and never wore it again.

> 'When Sylvia, Pamela and I joined Gayaza, it was a totally different experience. This was boarding school! We didn't like the rigidity and routine. We were not used to it. Every morning, we had to do chores like clean our dormitory and sweep the large compound. Each student was assigned a different chore every week. On Saturdays, we would peel *matoke*, the staple food which we had with pretty much every meal. Sundays, we

dressed up in white uniforms for a long church service where we sang hymns in both English and Luganda'.
—Norah Rwakihembo (Friend)

Part of Gayaza Primary School's original mission was to produce well-rounded young women who could function both in high-society and at home with their future husbands, friends, and family. For example, every Muganda lady should know how to prepare mashed green bananas, our traditional staple food. So, everyone had to learn to do that. Additionally, we were given early morning chores, which were distributed randomly as the supervisors or house mothers saw fit.

Luganda language classes were part of Gayaza Primary School curriculum. Granted most of us could speak it, but my friends and I were greatly challenged by that class. Although Luganda was my mother tongue, it wasn't for Norah and Pamela. The class ended after primary five. In hindsight, learning Luganda so intensely at such an early age during my formative years gave me mastery of the basics of my mother tongue and the language of my people.

'Unlike Lake Victoria School, Luganda was one of the subjects on the Gayaza syllabus, something we didn't really like and so I was actually surprised that Sylvia, Pamela and I passed the Luganda exams'.
—Norah Rwakihembo (Friend)

Life in Gayaza was no cakewalk. Our dormitories had to be kept meticulously clean. The layout was a mixture of some bunkbeds and single beds. At 6 a.m. precisely, we'd wake up to the *bugu*, a huge African drum that shook the entire campus.

First thing everyone did was to drop to their knees and say our morning prayers. Then we'd make our beds, and rush to the bathrooms, grab our buckets which already contained punishingly cold water, and quickly take baths, and thereafter complete our house chores before breakfast.

After breakfast, we'd all be sent to chapel to pray—again. Come to think of it, we did a lot of praying, all of which was mandatory. No one brought their children here if they didn't want them to engage in Christian norms and practices. Plainly put, Gayaza Primary School was an unapologetically Christian school.

Everything was carefully timed and regimented. There were consequences for any missteps with no exceptions. Teachers often used corporal punishment and toilsome chores (bathroom-scrubbing, banana-peeling, yard-cleaning) to exact compliance and adherence to the austere code of conduct. Boy were they strict!

> 'We would kneel to greet the matrons and other older people, something that wasn't common in our previous school. It was good to embrace our Kiganda culture'.
> –Norah Rwakihembo (Friend)

The only time of year we 'got back at them'—meaning our teachers—was on April Fool's Day, when we were allowed to prank them to a certain extent. I remember one April Fool's Day when some students created a white liquid paste out of starch and took it to the teachers and told them it was their milk. Thankfully no one fell for it. The teachers didn't find it funny to say the least.

In school I particularly loved English grammar, composition and what we called 'general paper' which I excelled in, but I struggled with mathematics. I was also active in sports, especially running and netball.

> 'Sylvia was a diligent student. In those days when the General Paper in the PLE exams could churn up questions from any topic under the sun, we all shared new knowledge and learnt from each other. I recall Sylvia telling me about a chap from ancient Greece, called Pheidippides, who ran non-stop to Athens to announce the Greek victory over the Persians. I came to appreciate her knowledge of current affairs which was well above the class average. Following the infamous 1976 Entebbe Raid by Israeli commandos, it was Sylvia who taught me the meaning of the term "Zionists"'.
>
> –Edi Kamya Mpanga (Friend)

Aside from Peace Kawalya, the tallest one of us who also made all the shots, I was also a star on the netball team until we met our match in Buddo Junior School, our archrival. They were the other premier primary school in the country. They beat us really bad! I'll never forget our coach Mr Dungu's after-game assessment: 'Sylvia, you didn't even touch the ball once'!

> 'Sylvia soon distinguished herself as a gifted sports person. She was an asset to the school team when it came to athletics, field events and netball. There was one skill my now good friend just could not muster. She couldn't sing to save her life! And all her efforts at its mastery during rehearsals invariably had everyone in stitches'.
>
> –Edi Kamya Mpanga (Friend)

Weekends were a mixed bag for me.

A neatly ironed and starched white dress and a red belt were our special uniform for church. I remember the excruciatingly long services when we'd literally sit for hours. I don't remember much of what was preached by the really passionate speakers, but during certain Sundays, almost the entire school would respond to invitations to commit our lives to God, only to forget it a couple of days later.

Saturday and Sunday afternoons were fun though. We'd sit and wait for our parents or guardians to bring us more grub. In a day without cellphones, we just had to wait and hope. They didn't send us arrival notifications or anything like that. I still remember that sunken let-down feeling when visiting hours ended without a visit from my family.

In those days, government boarding schools were the rave. They had the best teachers, so students performed better overall.

In my class, Dorah Nsubuga and my friend Edi Kamya always had the best grades. My other close friends were Rena Kyewalabye, Lydia Kavuma, Rita Sebalu, Florence Nakimera, Ann Kidza, Deborah Kaddu, Irene Sebowa and Miriam Mulira. Lydia's mother always brought lots of grub including home cooked food *(ekinumbo)*. And as Lydia's friend, I benefited from these eats a number of times, especially since my own parents were not regular visitors.

'My best memory with Sylvia is when we'd go looking for *"ebaluwa zobunyonyi"*(letters from birds) under one big tree behind Nasolo dormitory. We genuinely believed that the birds would deliver letters to announce our parents' visits. A fantasy of course, but it was everyone's hope that their parents would visit with grub during the weekend'.

    –Lydia Kavuma Zzinga Newest (Friend)

Starting school at Gayaza also meant moving in with Dad and Mummy Edith, my stepmom. Even though I was older and not resentful of Dad any more, I still didn't like it very much mainly because it separated me from my relatives and friends in Nkumba—the fun-happening place.

One day, I got an idea: What if I petitioned to be taken to Taata's house during the holidays, so I could play with the rest of the kids? I did. And it worked! As soon as school was up, I would spend a few days at home, and then he'd drive me to Nkumba, my favourite space.

Interestingly, every one of us kids were thinking the same thing. We'd all converge at the farm every holiday. Sometimes the house was so crowded with cousins, nephews, uncles, aunties that we could barely walk without stepping over something or bumping into someone.

To this day, I don't even know where we all slept, even with all the double-decker beds which Taata had purchased for us. We told funny stories, played all kinds of games, and ran around the perimeter of the compound from daybreak to dusk. It was fun!

'During the holidays, the Sebugwawo household was always filled with children with different personalities and interests. Sylvia amazingly got along very well

with pretty much all of us. We enjoyed many remarkably fun times together. She was ever humorous and
always enjoyed a good laugh. With a sparkle in her
eyes, she would keenly listen to my Congolese and
Swahili singing. Priceless'!

—Ann Loi Nangendo Fulu (Aunt)

As I progressed through the final years of primary school,
I started to notice my affinity to people. I really felt at home
around my friends: talking, laughing, cracking jokes, and playing games. I also liked pleasing people. I took it personally
when something I did had offended someone else. I felt deeply
responsible for others.

'We were young adolescents at the time. Looks and
body image were beginning to move to the forefront
of our thoughts. I remember noticing that my friend
was growing into a very pretty teenager, with beautiful
eyes set deep against her broad brow; her complex-
ion an attractive hue of brown. Never would I have
imagined that my warm-hearted friend would one day
become our regal Queen. What a privilege it is to have
known her in those days of childhood innocence'!

—Edi Kamya Mpanga (Friend)

## BOARDING SCHOOLS

Overall, I know I would not be the woman, mother, wife
and leader I am without that critical developmental time in
Gayaza Primary School.

Needless to say, life in boarding school was hard—perhaps too hard. We had a militaristic disciplinary culture, which the administration honestly believed helped make Gayaza Primary School the envy of any girl's school in East Africa. That said, I think that the potential scarring of some kids with certain personality types does not justify the no-doubt enormous academic benefits from these kinds of educational models. I believe that early enrolment into any boarding school removes kids from needed critical parental bonding which can potentially set them up for relationship dysfunction in adulthood.

However, I do believe that kids who are too sheltered, or kids who are not given the opportunity to develop social skills outside of their home environments also tend to exhibit dysfunctional relationship behaviour.

So, I say to parents who are reading this, love your kids, protect them, nurture them, grow them, educate them, but be ready to let them go and discover who they are. Indeed, they will always need your guidance; but more importantly, they will need to figure out their world. Is this easy? Of course not. To any loving mother, your child will always be your child, even when they're much older.

'As hard as Gayaza seemed then, I believe it made us the women we are today. I believe we were good students with great teachers, like our headmistress, Mrs Berry Jagwe. We learnt to be responsible at a young age. Etiquette and good manners were emphasised in the school. It was indeed a good foundation for us. To many of us who shared this formative process, it is no wonder that Sylvia became the Nnaabagereka of Buganda. I am extremely glad to have been a part of her life as she continues to steward this great role. When I see her on television, I am often tempted to call her and tell her how wonderful she looks or how great she speaks. I wish the Nnaabagereka a happy and peaceful long life and to be able to fulfil her role with continued greatness, as it has been written by the almighty God'.

—Norah Rwakihembo (Friend)

# chapter 4

# EBISOOMOOZA
## (Predicaments)

In 1966, Milton Obote, with the help of the military, attacked the palace of our king, Sir Edward Muteesa, completely desecrating the Buganda Kingdom and shattering its economy. Thousands lost their lives.

> 'I vividly recall when the Kabaka's palace was attacked on May 24, 1966. The Kabaka escaped unhurt from the palace but never returned. That incident bruised my heart that I still feel pain to this very day—it certainly took away my happiness and that of many other Baganda. He died in 1969'.
> —The Late Nelson Sebugwawo (Grandfather)

Taata carried a wound that I don't think any of us really understood. He lived a life of perpetual grief from the heart-breaking loss of his king and the cruel demise of our monarchy.

Five years later, on January 25, 1971, Idi Amin, the same military commander who had helped destroy the Buganda

Kingdom overthrew Milton Obote's government in a military coup. There were mass uprisings around the nation. The ire of frustration was aimed at those who had any political connections with Kabaka Yeka and UPC political parties. Taata had in some way been affiliated with both parties, and therefore he was in immediate danger.

## KULUGUUDO

When word of the coup reached our school, Lake Vic, parents started picking up their kids and in almost no time, the normally busy school was deserted. The driver took us straight to Taata's other home, Kuluguudo, because for some reason, the farmhouse was inaccessible. Once we got there, my grandma, Jajja Robinah, briefed us about the grim situation. She told us the villagers were organising to come and attack us. 'They claim Taata is an Obote supporter'! she added. I had no idea what she was talking about, since everyone knew how the Baganda hated Obote. The accusation was designed to incite outrage and justify maximum violence.

Jajja Robinah was defiant. 'This is my house. If they are going to kills us', she challenged, 'Let them go right ahead'. In our innocence, Nelson Kiraga and I got hold of our geometry sets, took out the dividers and pronounced that if they dared appear we will fight them with our weapons—we were ready for the showdown.

No sooner had we proclaimed our resistance, than my terrified Aunt Rose Mbewoze came running from the farmhouse to inform us that mobs had turned guns on to Taata and Maama, and that they were on their way to Kuluguudo to come after us. She pleaded that we should run away from the house and go hide somewhere.

Jajja Robinah grabbed us and led us away from the house. Fear gripped my heart as panic overtook us—it was me, Rose, Gladys, Robinah, Jennifer, Nelson, and Lydia. As we ran away, mobs of people were advancing towards our compound. I will never forget the jeers, the mocks, and the taunts of our neighbours. 'Hey you Sebugwawos, you are done'. We ignored them and kept running. Next thing I remember was Auntie Gladys grabbing my little hand…saying as she sobbed, 'Sylvia, let's go'. Though very scared, I obliged and kept on moving as we frantically manoeuvred through the bushes towards the main street in the hope of catching a ride to Kampala city, twenty-five miles away.

We suddenly stopped and converged in a nearby bush adjacent to the main road. Then Jajja Robinah decided she was going to head back to the house regardless of the situation. 'Please don't go! They will kill you'! We all pleaded, but it was clear she was not persuadable.

As she proceeded toward the house, she instructed us, *'Mwe kakati mugende ku Lukooto'*, meaning, 'Y'all should head out to Lukooto'. This is near Kampala where her cousins lived.

*But how do we get there?*

The roads were deserted. We were scared. We couldn't hitch-hike all the way there. It was too far. We had to catch a ride to the city. We flagged down the first car, but as soon as he saw the lot of us, he sped away.

Just then, there came another car, an old Peugeot 504, which we desperately flagged down. Like the first driver, he stopped hesitatingly. We asked, *'Bambi tutwale e Kampala'?* meaning, 'Will you please take us to Kampala'? we begged. He was reluctant, but thankfully he agreed on condition that all the little ones sit on the floor of the car with their heads down to avoid being seen.

Somehow, all seven of us squeezed into the back of that sedan, and off to the big city we went. Aunt Rose, probably in her early twenties; Gladys and Robinah, teenagers; Nelson age 10, me, at nine years old; Jennifer age 7, and 5-year-old Lydia. He graciously drove us past the military check points all the way to Lukooto which is located in Mengo.

We were greeted with warm embraces from our aunties who were surprised to see us. Since we didn't have cellphones at the time, we were left to our wildest imaginations as to what was going on back in Kuluguudo and at the farm in Nkumba.

My auntie Rose decided not to stay at Lukooto but instead travel to my dad's place at Mulago to inform him of the tragic developments including our grandparents' arrest.

Even still, my young mind could not fathom the outrage.

## SAINT LUKE'S CHURCH

As the days rolled on, news of Taata's situation finally reached our desperate ears.

The angry mob had pillaged and burned down the house at Kuluguudo. Their mission was to destroy everything. Others threatened to slaughter the whole family. Fortunately, news had reached our relatives (Uncles Fred Bamundaga, Abraham Muzinga and Stephen Bulega, who were serving in the military) in time for them to mobilise and hastily dispatched a unit to protect the rest of Taata's estate. Apart from a few missing cows, the family was saved from what undoubtedly could have been a bloody tale of angry mob justice.

As the political transition took hold, people calmed down. It was time to return home.

Back at the farm, when Maama saw me, she was so happy. She literally took me to her bedroom to make sure I was unharmed. Then she did something I will never forget—she walked away for a few minutes, and returned with a boiled egg, and asked me to eat it. It was a token of her enduring love for me. In a way, she was saying, 'I am so glad you are well. I am so glad you are in my life'!

With Kuluguudo destroyed, Jajja Robinah and all her children moved to the farmhouse in Nkumba to stay with us.

'After grandpa's other house was destroyed during Obote's ouster, he decided to move everyone under the same roof while it was being rebuilt. There were kids everywhere, including the farmhands' and helpers' kids too. I remember the dance competitions in the living room. Top prize would go to whoever did the Apollo 11 dance the best. Sylvia always had to win…'.

–Fred Lutalo (Cousin)

Taata was a good man. He was kind and ever so generous, always desiring the best for others. He was also a devout Protestant. He would later build Saint Luke's Church, a flagship Anglican church in Nkumba. I will never forget his words after he completed the church. He declared, *'Kati nebweenfa'*, meaning, 'I am now ready to die'! By God's grace, he lived another decade or so.

Years later, I was invited to speak at a family gathering at that very church. As I recounted the horrible events of that terrible day in 1971, how close we had all come to total extermination, sitting right in front of me was one of the leaders of that mob. He must have been ninety years old. Clearly, he was remorseful. His was an act of redemption. I felt compassion for him. Thank God I had long forgiven him.

## WANYANGE GIRLS SECONDARY SCHOOL

Our final exam, commonly known as the Primary Leaving Examinations or PLEs were fast approaching, and it was time for us to select our choices for applications to secondary school. Ordinarily, it was compulsory for Gayaza Primary School students to select Gayaza High School as their first choice. However, in our year, that rule was relaxed. Parents allowed their kids to choose whichever school they desired.

Taata and Dad were both handling my education affairs. Taata was also on the Parent Teacher Association of Gayaza High School. Yet, they together decided to select Budo Kings College as my first choice, Wanyange Girls School my second choice, and two other schools. Gayaza High School was omitted from their list. To this day, I'm not sure why they choose that way.

When the results came back, I had passed well with an A grade which would have seen me accepted to Gayaza High School, but my first choice, Budo, had a much higher passing grade. Taata and Dad decided to send me to my second choice: Wanyange Girls Secondary School. This wasn't very good news to me, going so far away from home when most of my friends stayed within Buganda region for their secondary school education.

Wanyange Girls School is located in Busoga (another recognised traditional institution) in the eastern part of Uganda in Jinja district. I remember Taata taking us to Jinja to visit a relative and see the famous Owen Falls Dam. It was a fun ride, with many of us in the car talking loudly and reading out road signposts as we passed them. Taata was great at entertaining children!

But this was a different story, I was being taken to a boarding school far from home where I would spend months at a time. This was to be my first time away from everybody I knew. I was pensive and sad, thinking what it all meant to me.

Wanyange Girls was a popular school which attracted bright students from across the nation. It is located in Busoga on Nyange Hill overlooking the beautiful Lake Victoria. It is no wonder the guerilla fighters found it militarily strategic during the 1979 war that overthrew Idi Amin Dada.

I distinctly remember that first trip like it was yesterday. It was just the two of us in Dad's light blue Toyota Corolla.

We didn't say much to each other, just the long buzzing sound of the car. We set off from our house at Kololo (Plot No. 3 K.A.R Drive, Lower Kololo Terrace), on to Jinja Road going east through Namanve and Mabira Forests, passed Lugazi Sugar Plantations. It seemed like an endless journey. Back then, there wasn't much activity along Jinja Road. I sat quietly in the car as I looked out pondering what was ahead for me. We eventually crossed the bridge at the Owen Falls Dam, passed the road to Jinja town, as we approached Bugembe township.

Then, we turned off the main road and drove on a dusty dirt road for a while until we reached a steep hill. I wondered if the car would make it up there. Just as soon as it reached the top, we hit a sudden drop, so much so that I was afraid the car was going to tip over. I am sure Dad was nervous too although he wouldn't let me see it. Meanwhile, I am petrified. *No wonder I didn't want to come this far*, I thought. I murmured, though under my breath, 'Where are we going'? Dad didn't turn his head once.

Finally we approached the school gate, perhaps a slight, strange relief. I wondered what kind of school this was. The commute alone was exasperating. Thankfully the road was reconstructed the following year, making it easier for cars to access. Wanyange was a very clean and orderly school, in spite of its remote location. Their structures were well maintained; the compound lush and well kept.

Meryl Haden, a white elderly English lanky woman, was the headmistress of the school. She had been in the local school system for many years and was about to retire when I enroled at Wanyange. She was known for her strictness and feared by many for her stern approach. Age was catching up to Ms Haden. She was losing her memory, which made her the brunt of many a veiled joke. She was known to forget students' faces and names. Sometimes she'd ask misbehaving students to follow her to her office or residence to be punished. On the way over, the culprits would often sneak away and escape. They didn't think much of the consequences since Ms Haden would not remember who it was, so they'd get away.

Mrs Turyahikayo was the deputy headmistress. She was much younger and alert, perhaps by design so she could make up for Ms Haden's deficits. She hailed from Western Uganda; slim, medium height, with dark chocolate skin. She always had the perfect posture. She walked straight with heels together, as if she had been through military training. She was a no-nonsense disciplinarian who was quick to punish misbehaviour, sometimes indiscriminatingly whipping students with little cause. She would later be promoted to headmistress. Suffice to say, in hindsight, both of these women were critical to my academic journey in inestimable ways.

## ABAYAAKA (NEWCOMERS)

Newcomers were received by their new housemothers and the older girls. I was assigned to a girl named Margret Kitakule, who was two years ahead of me in senior three. Her job was to help me settle in. She took both of my suitcases, the one with clothes and the other with grub, from the car to inside the dormitory. She helped me make my bed—top bunk bed, commonly designated to the newbies. The large dorm also had single beds in the cubical that slept ten-twelve students. We were assigned lockers to keep our grub and other essential items. Margret kept some of my grub in her locker.

Kids from Kampala were popular. We had a little more grub than those coming from within Busoga and other parts of Eastern Uganda. So, consequently, we were more attractive to the older girls.

At Wanyange Girls, I had many friends including Ruth Nabeta, Robinah Nalubega, Lydia Nakatude, Deborah Lukwago, Aisha Mohammed, Immaculate Uwayirigira, Rose Nakafeero, Harriet Mpagi-Kagwa, Betty Nambi, Elsie Mukasa, Rose Ibale, Rachel Ssesanga, Winnie Nsadha, Joyce Ibanda, Christine Umutonyi, and Nakato Katto.

'Almost right away we connected, even though she was in a class below me. We were both from Kampala. There was this unspoken code between us, the big-city girls. The general assumption was that we were classier and generally more refined. Her pace was slower as she was more pensive and calculated, while I was more outgoing. She did not just simply jump because everyone else did, which made me that much more curious about her'.
—Lydia Nakatude Sserebe (Friend)

Newcomers were dubbed *bayaaka* or *abayaaka*, meaning 'new' in Lusoga. There was a hazing ritual or an initiation ceremony that *abayaaka* went through on their very first night in school. The older girls would verbally assault them, eat their grub, confiscate their belongings, pour water all over them, and beat them up.

In their minds, they genuinely thought it was a fun way of saying, 'Welcome to Wanyange'. Unfortunately, the bullying was by no means victimless. Some newcomers quit the school, while others carried those scars well into adulthood.

Luckily, I wasn't bullied because Margret, being one of the bullies, protected me. She was feared, so no one touched me. I guess her payoff was my grub, which she would easily access without my consent. It wasn't a bad deal considering what fellow *bayaakas* had to go through.

That first day, I also met Ruth Nabeta, who would become one of my best friends. She slept in a different dormitory, but somehow Margret also took care of her and protected her possibly because her family—the Nabetas—were a prominent family in Busoga.

> 'We got to Wanyange Girls School as young lost souls in a big new world. Initially, Sylvia and I were desk-mates. As events continued to connect us, we would develop a lifelong friendship. I remember sitting at the sailing club in Jinja feeling like we were queens of the whole world. During the holidays, we made it a point to visit each other's homes. I have so many special memories with her. We also got into so much trouble together… I remember getting caught in her dormitory after lights out one night. The following day, I was punished with a chore—to dig ten, 3-metre holes. She was like a sister to me. I really miss those good old days'.
>
> —Ruth Nabeta (Friend)

The daily school routine at Wanyange was not much different from most boarding schools in Uganda at that time. The overarching goal was clear: We receive an academic education while also learning to gain personal independence, so ultimately, we are able to function in society by taking care of ourselves, others and our surroundings.

Even with the excellence in cleanliness and maintenance, it was our responsibility to keep the school clean and tidy throughout the day, week and school term. There were five dormitories. Our sleeping space had to always be in order. Every Saturday, the house mothers would inspect all the dormitories and rate them. It was incumbent upon each one of us to see that ours is the best. Frankly speaking, I'm not sure how they rated our performance. It seemed to me that we were all excellent.

Equally, our bodies had to look presentable. It was mandatory to bathe twice every day. Our hair had to be kept short and neat. Our uniforms clean and ironed.

While other secondary schools, like Gayaza where I wanted to go, allowed their senior girls to have socials with boys' schools, Wanyange didn't. All outings were strictly prohibited. We hated the isolation, especially since the school was within proximity of other top tier schools such as Mwiri Boys College.

I remember when Jinja College boys came for a debate session with us. Immediately after the debate, the boys were instructed to get on their bus and leave. Fortunately, I got to greet them personally since I headed the debate club. Everybody was bummed out.

'I have known Sylvia since primary school in Gayaza. During holidays, she would come to our house to play. Some of her relatives were friends with my siblings. Our lives would re-converge two years later when we both joined Wanyange for secondary school. Although she was two classes ahead of me, I immensely enjoyed spending time with her.'

—Justine Nakato Katto (Friend)

## SUSPENSION

Being located on top of a hill, we constantly had water issues. The water pump was inadequate to push the thousands of liters of water needed to meet our needs.

One day, it stopped. Yes, not one drop! The school corralled us to the odious task to take our buckets, march down to the well in Bugembe town centre and carry the water uphill to our dorms.

We were thrilled, or at least I was! Now keep in mind that Wanyange was run like a prison camp. Once in, we never got out until our parents or guardians came to pick us up at the end of the school term. Any impermissible disappearance, or what was called 'a French leave', was subject to immediate expulsion.

Once we got to the water well, we couldn't resist the temptation to visit the small shops. We didn't have any money on us, so we couldn't even buy anything. We just wanted to taste the freedom, completely oblivious to the dire consequences of our curious escapade.

Upon our return from the well, we could almost smell the trouble. Our names had been shortlisted for disciplinary action. We were charged with absconding from school. That was the biggest offence. It was a total dereliction of our student obligations and was often punishable by immediate expulsion.

Knowing this, I decided to get ahead of the ensuing problem. I suggested to Ruth and Robinah Nalubega, my friends, that since the administration hadn't yet decided what to do with us, we should pre-emptively protest any harsh punishment as mistreatment. We were thinking of planning a strike. Well, we chickened out. All twenty-five of us were placed on a two-week immediate suspension from school. I freaked out. I was staying with Dad and my stepmom, Mummy Edith at the time. How was I going to explain why I was home in the middle of the school term? Telling them the truth was definitely out of the question. They would kill me!

Thankfully, Dad was on a training trip in Italy, so I felt confident enough to sell Mummy Edith on some tall tale about being bullied, and how I really wanted to immediately transfer to a different school, Makerere College. She bought it, but he didn't, well not the whole tall tale. So, I made a deal with Mummy Edith, 'Okay, let me stay home for now. You will take me back in time for exams'.

'Sure, you can stay, but no loitering. You will stay here in the house the entire time'! she replied.

I kept my end of the deal but decided to raid my dad's book collection; and for the entire two weeks, I was like a sponge. I read over a dozen novels, mostly by James Hadley Chase. In fact, I started having dreams of the different characters that enchanted my young imagination.

Dad and Mummy Edith were good readers; Dad's book cabinet was stacked with novels by English authors. He had no problem with me reading the novels. In fact, he encouraged it. However, trouble came when I let my friends borrow novels without his permission. You see, reading was 'the thing' for us. We exchanged novels among us. This works out well if the borrower doesn't lend the novel to someone else whom you don't know, so you never see it again. I worked hard to make sure that never happened to any of Dad's novels.

Eventually, it was time to return to Wanyange. There was a snag. You see, a suspension of this nature required that my father should personally take me back to school. Since he wasn't home, I had to take one of my uncles, but that meant that he would find out about my delinquency and report it to my parents. I wasn't going to let that happen. I decided to contact Uncle Steven Bulega. He was much younger, and totally laidback.

When the school headmistress saw him, she was unconvinced and sent me back into suspension. 'Go get your father or you will be expelled indefinitely'! she demanded.

I had to take Uncle Ziiki Kiryowa Kulubya, one of Dad's closest friends, and much as I tried to keep my mess under wraps, it exploded in my face. I was lashed for my deception and certainly never forgot about it to this very day.

# A PIVOTAL SEASON

I would spend four years at Wanyange.

As I look back upon my journey, I consider my time there to be something of a divine appointment. So much of who I am today was determined by those years. It is there that I made such great memories and many wholesome lifelong friendships.

'We were in the same dorm. Unlike most of the girls there, she was open, generous, and friendly. When other kids talked about their parents, Sylvia and I couldn't relate because we were both raised by our grandparents. That drew us even closer. One day, she received a package from her mother in the USA. It was a cassette player, along with several tapes. The school didn't allow items like that in the dorms, so one of our teachers, Mrs Wayoto agreed to keep it for her. She promised to allow us to listen to the music on the weekends. So every Saturday, we made it a point to go listen to the Bee Gee's, Jackson 5, Diana Ross, and many more. The lull of the music left us on a high, so to keep from plummeting into depression on account of our starkly different reality, we had dream sessions together. We dreamt the wildest dreams of preferred futures. That time became a highlight for us each weekend'.

–Robinah Nalubega Mukasa (Friend)

If you asked me at the time, I would have probably preferred to have continued my education at Gayaza High School. But God had something else in mind for me.

First of all, our school had much stricter codes of conduct and ethics, so I was both tutored and groomed differently than I would have at Gayaza High School, which was more liberal. Second, Wanyange was a school with markedly greater tribal diversity. That pushed me out of my cocoon to begin to inter-relate, understand and appreciate other rich cultures that our great nation is so blessed with. This would later broaden and augment my service to my country beyond my role as Nnaabagereka in the Kingdom of Buganda.

> 'Being a late entrant in my first boarding school, I was scared and alone. She saw me and gently approached me. She spoke Luganda, my mother tongue, which was comforting since most of the girls in Wanyange didn't. Sylvia made me feel safe and accepted. In her, I found a friend. We dreamt together and made many memories during our time there… Hers was the only home my parents would allow me to visit during the holidays. They believed she was a good influence on me. I was always impressed by her simplicity. She had chores, just like I did, even if her family could afford house-help'.
>
> —Deborah Lukwago Alibu (Friend)

I didn't want to do any sports in Wanyange, even though I was a great runner. Somehow, I was drawn to cerebral activities like the debate club, which woke up the thinker within. I also joined the drama club, and the fashion club which I later headed. I became good at articulating facts and defending positions, which has been an invaluable discipline affecting every aspect of what I do today.

'I was the short, new kid who was easy prey for the big bullies at Wanyange. She stood up for me and told them to back off. They did! Instantly, we connected and would forge a strong, lifelong friendship. Sylvia was always smartly dressed. While our uniforms got soiled from the grind, hers looked like she'd just put it on. She was also a champion of the underdog... The teachers noticed her reading skills and designated her classroom reader. Sylvia was excellent in English grammar, mostly because she was relentless. Additionally, her allocution skills gave her a leg up in the school debate club. She strived in mathematics pondering each problem for hours, as though her quest was deeply personal. Although she wasn't musically inclined, she could dance! To this day, Sylvia will bust a move if given the chance'.

—Harriet Mpagi-Kagwa (Friend)

# chapter 5

# OKUNUNULWA
## (Liberation)

In 1972, Idi Amin expelled 80,000 Asians from the country. That shattered the economy and plunged Uganda into utter chaos. Consequently, political repression, tribal persecution, and nepotism became the norm. Notable civil servants, clergy, and anyone deemed a threat to the government was oppressed. Dissent was deadly as hundreds of thousands of citizens were extra-judicially slaughtered. Sharia Law was quickly replacing Christianity as Amin desired to turn Uganda away from the West and its ideals, into an Islamic republic. The country experienced a severe brain-drain as thousands of its learned citizens fled into exile for safety.

## LIBERATED

In 1979, A Tanzania-based army launched a historic march upon the capital city to oust the deranged dictator.

Unfortunately for us, the war intensified while we were in school. As Amin's soldiers were being driven out of major cities, they started to commit atrocities. We were afraid. The school administration was also afraid. As they were grappling for direction, it was announced that the capital city, Kampala, had been cut off.

The school administration at Wanyange abruptly sent everyone back to their homes, but we, the Kampala-city girls could not leave, as the main artery into the capital city had been cut off. We knew that the situation was bleak; there was hardly any food left in the kitchen, with no end of this brutal war in sight. Those students who could, were free to leave school—particularly those who lived in Busoga and farther east. Parents came in big numbers to take their children home, as others walked away by themselves.

Since we were stuck in school and had a measure of skepticism about the severity of the situation, we decided to take a stroll into the main town, Jinja and take a closer look. Seas of both civilians and military personnel were on the main Jinja-Mbale Highway heading farther east, fleeing the fighting. Cars were racing through town carrying the more well-to-do, including Idi Amin's political allies. There was heavy traffic along with people carrying their belongings. We managed to cross the main highway heading towards Jinja town, but stopped and decided that we should head back to school.

As we waited to cross the highway again, I saw a familiar face in the back seat of one of the cars. This lady looked pensive and troubled. As I looked closer, our eyes met as they sped by and drove her off. It was Auntie Gladys. *No…it can't be her,* I thought. *It must be someone else.* I couldn't stop seeing that pensive looking lady in the back seat of that car. Was it really Auntie Gladys?

Indeed, it was her I saw that day. Evidently, she did see me and had pondered on whether to stop and pick me up but decided not to. They would face grievous challenges on their ill-fated escape from Kampala. Had I jumped into that car with them, it is highly probable that my family would have never seen me again.

As the liberation forces approached Jinja, with the sound of bombardment within hearing range, dread griped our school. We had never heard of such loud thuds before.

*'Abakomboozi batuse'!* someone announced. Meaning, 'The liberation fighters have arrived'. The fighters included Tanzanians and Ugandans who had gone into exile. At this point they were liberating Jinja town and the neighbouring townships and villages, but we had no idea that they would come up to our school.

The bombing continued for some days, and then one afternoon our school was overrun by the Bakomboozi. We were terrified. As we started to scream, they quickly told us that they were harmless. They managed to calm us down and promised to protect us from fleeing insurgents.

Apparently, they had decided to camp out in our school because it was strategically suited for their purposes. From there, they could see what was happening in Jinja and other neighbouring areas.

Our new guests camped out on our school grounds; and since we were convinced that they were harmless, we decided to go and have a chat with them.

We asked them questions about the war. We checked out their weapons and we even asked to touch their guns. They showed us bullets and hand grenades. Yes, we actually had a cordial conversation with the Bakomboozi. One of them said that he was a student at university and had left to fight for a cause that he strongly believed in.

That night when we went to sleep, some girls started conversations on how they had heard stories of students being raped by army men. We laughed it off as we drifted to sleep. Later that night, we were awakened by a girl screaming. 'The men are here'! she shrieked. We hid under our beds while holding on to each other for dear lives as the Bakomboozi gained entrance into our dormitory.

'They are going to rape us and kill us'! screamed one of the other girls. That sent the whole dorm into a panic. We screamed at the top of our lungs. Two of the soldiers calmly said, *'Pole, pole bwana', meaning,* 'It's okay…calm down'! They said they were checking on us to make sure we were okay. That wasn't as convincing as the first time. If they had any dark intentions that night, our deafening screams must have held them back.

One thing is for sure, these were nothing like Amin's goons. They were not the intimidating soldiers that we were used to seeing. They even spoke a different, gentler-sounding dialect of Swahili. You see, Swahili was the language of the army.

We associated it with violence. To most of us, it was the preferred language of subjugation by the military, police, and pretty much all of law enforcement.

The invading army would capture and liberate the city of Jinja, the nation's industrial base. Next up was Mbale, which they easily overran as they advanced north to liberate the rest of Uganda from Idi Amin's brutal regime.

We didn't fully understand what had transpired, except that we were terrified and just wanted to go home. We longed to see our loved ones. Eventually, the administration allowed us to leave, but with public transport at a standstill, we were trapped. It felt as though we were stuck in a bad experiment.

## A TRAIN RIDE

Just then, one of the girls mentioned that there was a train we could take to Kampala. Unlike the roads, railway tracks were still open. We jumped right on the idea. None of us had experienced rail travel, but we agreed to take our chances. With no end in sight to the unrest, we felt that this was the only functional means of transportation back to our families. The school staff that had been left in charge agreed to this plan. We would take the rest of the day to pack as little as possible and prepare for the trek to Kampala at the break of the following day.

'We had agreed to travel light, but true to form, Sylvia shows up with a large suitcase filled with her belongings. We tried to explain to her why this was a bad idea, and how we needed to be light on our feet on account of the long, uncertain commute ahead, but she would not budge. I could see that determined look in her eye. Negotiations were futile, so we relented'.

—Harriet Kagwa (Friend)

Soon we were chugging away in a crowded, old, slow, dirty, rinky-dink train. We didn't care much though. We were finally headed home. And guess what we used as our makeshift pillow in the toilsome ride? The big suitcase I was not supposed to have.

The all-night journey took us straight to the city centre, the Kampala Train Station. We were exhausted but grateful. Unfortunately, it was too early for us to walk home that morning. With law and order pretty much down the drain, the deserted Kampala streets were frightening to say the least. We had to wait until daylight at the station.

After the sun came up, I managed to persuade the station master to allow me to call home. Our families had not heard from us in months. They feared the worst. Dad promptly rushed out to come pick me up in an unfamiliar car. I was on the lookout for his beloved Toyota Corolla. Boy did he love that car! Well, it turns out that his car had been stolen by fleeing Amin soldiers.

Life would slowly return back to normal and we went back to school. I just had to complete a couple more school terms at Wanyange before graduating from senior four, my last year there. At that time Wanyange didn't have seniors five and six.

I still remember the long car ride back from my last day at Wanyange. Unlike my first day with just Daddy and me, he rode with Uncle Jimmy Mitanda to pick me up. It was then that I learnt of the loss of one of my uncles, Saulo Muyingo. Apparently, he had vanished, never to be seen again. I was devastated because Uncle Saulo was very dear and close to me. I remember him coming home almost every day. His wife, a Russian lady, Aunty Galina, was so kind to me, and I loved all his children so dearly. The thought that someone that close can be here one day and gone the next haunted me. This tragedy devastated Maama at Nkumba. Uncle Saulo was her fourth born son. The next day, I was on my way to Nkumba to see her. For months and years to come we would grieve for Uncle Saulo. Since his body was never found, for long we hoped that maybe he would show up one day.

I would spend the next few months of that long after-high school vacation mostly at Nkumba and partly with Dad and Mummy Edith in Kololo. The lull allowed me time to ponder the big lessons that my young life was inviting me to consider. The woman in me was learning how to survive and thrive in the midst of unpredictability and chaos. God was forming inside me the critical ability to interpret events and to glean life lessons from them.

'I have had the honour of walking with Sylvia through some of the most significant seasons of her life. From our teenage years in Uganda, to her times in the United States, we have walked through happy, sad, bad and good times. I starkly remember our visits in Kololo at Plot 3 K.A.R Drive, or at her school in Wanyange, and even later during her visits to London. We read novels, shared secrets, and walked through some really trying times like when my mother passed away'.

—Sarah Kiyingi-Kaweesa (Cousin)

## UTTER CHAOS

During the long vacation before what we called higher school, I learnt that my mother who had immigrated to the USA from the UK, wanted me to join her. She had processed a residency permit (Green Card) which had been approved by the US embassy in Kampala. Seemingly overnight, I was thrust upon an entirely different course of my life journey. Yes, I was going to the United States of America.

'I didn't want to disrupt her high school education because Jajja Nelson had her in some of the best schools in the country. After she had completed senior four, I felt it was time, so I applied for a green card for her to join me in New York. My application was approved, and my daughter was on her way to me'.

—Rebecca Musoke (Mother)

'You know what, Deborah? When I go to America, I am going to get really serious with my life. I am going to work very hard'. Anxious words soberly spoken to my childhood friend Deborah Lukwago who had come to visit me at my dad's house in Kololo a few days before I left. The prospect of what would undoubtedly be a major transitional moment was somewhat daunting and sobering.

Dad and Mummy Edith threw a farewell party for me that March. Friends, relatives and well-wishers came to bid me farewell and celebrate my next chapter.

It was 1981. The political climate in Uganda was deteriorating. The country had plummeted into anarchy once again. Factions of the army had banded together to terrorise villages. Military generals acted like inner-city drug lords with absolute power. Rapes and indiscriminate killings were the norm. It seemed as though one of Uganda's cheap commodities was life.

Nights were terrifying. I distinctly remember one horrid night when we were awakened by gunshots in the neighbour's house. Armed thugs had come to kill the head of the home. *'Onzise'!* (meaning, 'You've killed me'!), yelled his son. Then I heard a series of bone-chilling screams from a woman's voice. I hid under my bed and stayed there till morning.

At the crack of dawn, we went to see what had happened, and indeed the young man's body was lying in their neighbour's backyard—he had been shot as he tried to escape. His father, who had hidden from his killers in the attic, was violently sobbing. The whole neighbourhood was in shock.

Shortly thereafter, Dad placed a huge metallic burglar door and added electric fencing around the house. But that didn't do much for me. I was still traumatised. I kept hearing the penetrating screams from our neighbour's family. I kept seeing that dead body. I kept seeing the shadow of this one man who had tried to break into our home through my window. I dreaded nighttime; so for weeks, I would sneak down under my bed to sleep there all night. It's where I felt safe.

News of the return of ex-president Milton Obote who had previously persecuted our family was unsettling to me, and the entire tribe. We held him responsible for the death of our king and the ultimate demise of the Buganda Kingdom.

As you can imagine, the thought of finally leaving all this behind to emigrate to the USA was immensely comforting on one hand—but sad and frightening on another because I was leaving my family, friends and home behind.

## FAREWELL SYLVIA

'Right after high school, her biological mother, Rebecca, suggested that she should go live with her in America. We were sad to see her go, but happy for her. She would meet and learn to love her real mother'.

—John Luswata (Father)

Before I left, I wanted to physically bid my maternal grandparents, George and Norah Musoke, who lived in Kirondo Nazigo farewell. My dad encouraged me to go there and see them.

Even though I could only vaguely remember how to get there—I hadn't been there in ten years—I somehow thought I'd make my way out there on my own.

Off to Mukono I went. Jumping in and out of taxis, from town to town, asking for directions until I got to what I thought was the final stop. There I got walking directions to my grandparents' house. Thankfully, everyone knew who they were. It is customary for people to know each other in an African village.

I walked for what felt like hours. Folks along the way were kind enough to direct me to stick to the *murrum* dirt road which ran through a thick forest. I walked through the forest along a narrow path of valleys amid swamps. At 18 years old, I was totally petrified. They kept saying, 'Oh it's just down the road...keep walking'. Quite a typical response if I might say.

I did make it. When I walked into Grandfather's house through the back door of their home, everyone was shocked. They couldn't believe I had travelled so far on my own. Just then I started to realise the danger of my adventure. With bands of violent militias indiscriminately killing people and committing atrocities around the back hills of the district, I could have been raped or worse. After the formal greetings, they explained to me that I could have taken another taxi right to their front door.

I hastily broke the news of my upcoming departure for America. For several days we talked, dined, and laughed together as they prepared to send me back to Kololo.

'*Beeka mutulabire'* (meaning, 'Please greet Rebecca for us') they chorused as they bid me goodbye. Mum's younger brother, Uncle Lubowa, took me to the train station. They were not about to take any chances with my commute again. I could tell that they really missed my mother. Besides a couple of my aunties who had also immigrated to the United States, Mum had successfully broken through the thick ceiling of poverty to create a better life experience for herself. They called her lucky! And I was going to live with her. Indeed, I felt blessed.

'We were sad to see her go to the USA. I remember her farewell party at Kololo, and the drive to the airport. She had to go and spend time with her biological mother. Months later, I received a letter from her saying that she was missing us, which made me real sad. She was fortunate to have three mothers: Jajja who nurtured her through her early years  and took care of her during her formative years, myself, and Rebecca who birthed her'.

—Mummy Edith Luswata (Stepmom)

# OKWEZIMBA
## (Self-Empowerment)

'Kola Ng'omuddu Olye Ng'omwami'
(Luganda Proverb)

Translation:
*'Work Like a Slave and You'll Eat Like a Lord'*

# AMERIKA
## (America)

On March 22, 1981, I boarded the Sabena Airlines flight to Brussels via Rwanda and Burundi. I remember seeing my dad tearing up as he bid me farewell. I had never seen him like that. I remember his warm embrace. The night before, he had handed me a twenty-dollar bill for trip pocket money. Everything was so new. It would be my first time to fly.

The European leg of the flight was excruciatingly long. I was seated next to a kind white man who was curious about the young passenger next to him. 'Where are you going'? he asked. 'To join my mother in America'! With every question, I had ten answers. I must have talked his head off, but he seemed to take interest in everything I said; he must have noticed the excitement and anticipation in my eyes. I remember him handing me his pen to write with and keep. He must have felt badly for me after seeing me frantically trying to fruitlessly write with my old pen. I wanted to make entries in my notepad that Uncle Lubowa had just given me. I could almost feel the future screaming at me.

# 'SORRY, YOU ARE IN THE WRONG LINE'

Brussels was freezing. I had never felt that cold in my entire life. Clearly, I was ill prepared for the chilly stopover. In those days, the airlines provided accommodations for overnight layovers. I remember being shuttled to the hotel. I felt like I was in a dream.

The hotel was comfortable, but the night was very short. In the morning, the shuttle dropped me off at the terminal and what an overwhelming sight! There were signs everywhere. Los Angeles, New York, London, Cairo…

Finally, I got into what I thought was my check-in lane to New York. The line was so long.

After what seemed like forever, I got to the ticketing desk. 'You are in the wrong line. There is your line', said an attendant as she pointed vigourously to a line in the distance. I promptly rushed over there and stood in another long line as I waited patiently for my turn. As soon as I got to the desk, the attendant announced, 'It's too late. You see your flight is now closed. You can't get on. You will need to wait until the next flight tomorrow morning'!

Shock, trepidation, and extreme anxiety rushed through my cold body. *Wait…I can't stay. What do I do now?* I froze, right there in the massive airport lobby tightly hugging my bags. I remember thinking about the *matooke* (green bananas) in the bag that I was taking to New York for my mother. Boy was that bag heavy!

Minutes turned into hours. I kept walking between gates, climbing escalators between terminals, and rambling to myself,

*What are you going to do now, Sylvia? You can't go back to the hotel. You are stuck.* I was helpless and totally clueless. No one was there to guide me. Perhaps a call to the Ugandan Embassy would have helped, but I didn't think about it then.

When I asked for help at the information counter, they pointed me to the train and advised me to find a student hostel outside the airport. They spoke French and didn't care that I could not understand what they were saying. They seemed completely heartless, brisk and discourteous. I kept thinking about my twenty dollars. Maybe that will help here. I was desperate.

I thought I should leave and look for a hostel outside the airport. As I stepped onto the escalator to the train terminal, I heard, 'Hello, where are you going? I've been watching you all day as you walked up and down this whole terminal. What's going on'? I was so relieved. There she was, my guardian 'angel' in the form of a kind Filipino woman named Audrea Aquino.

'I missed my flight, so now I am going to look for a place to stay. I have been told to catch a train to take me there', I replied.

'Well, I think I have a better idea. I have a friend from Rwanda here in Brussels who might be able to let us stay with him tonight'. Wow. God had totally made a way out for me. I don't know what I would have done. I later learnt that the $20 was too little to cover my transportation, food and housing for the night.

Audrea knew exactly where to go. By the time we got there, the wind chill had cut through my little sweater. I was frozen to the bone. Her Rwandese friend, Andre Senga, did let us stay the night, and what a kind heart he was!

In New York, my mother was in sheer panic. Her daughter was not on the flight from Brussels as they anticipated. After hours of waiting and searching through the airport arrival paperwork, they informed her that I didn't leave Brussels. When they called the airport, no one knew where I was.

Meanwhile, the following morning we hastened to return to the Brussels airport to check in for our flights. I was so thankful for my 'angel'. We kept in touch with Andre and especially Audrea for years after that frightful night.

I did get on the flight that morning and flew to New York on March 24.

JFK. Wow! What a huge airport compared to Uganda's Entebbe International Airport. I had never seen anything like it. The crowds, the nationalities, the buzz of US customs and immigration—all overwhelmed my senses.

My green card (or permanent residence status) was expeditiously processed at the airport, and I was admitted to the United States of America.

With no bags to claim, I was anxious to see my mother. Excited as I was to be with her, I was a bit disappointed that there wasn't more besides the outward relief of a long journey travelled and a destination reached. I suppose I had underestimated the impact of the physical separation between us. She was pregnant with Monique, my baby sister.

Mother handed me a heavy warm jacket and we proceeded to the exit. It was cold, but not as bad as Brussels. She flagged down a yellow cab and we jumped in. As we drove out of JFK to Roosevelt Island, I couldn't help but marvel at the unfolding story of my life.

# SETTLING IN

Life in America wasn't rosy at the out start. I felt like I was living with strangers.

First, there was a mother I hardly knew; then a 4-year-old brother I had never met, and a stepfather. Yes, my mother married a wonderful man from Ghana named Maxwell Codjoe who tried very hard to make me feel comfortable.

> 'I was only 4 years old when she joined our family. I was immediately drawn to her. I remember her when my baby sister was born. I remember her taking me to school. I remember her protecting me, playing with me and hanging out with me. Sylvia was my big sis… simple as that'.
>
> –Reuben Codjoe (Brother)

We lived in a two-bedroom house. I shared a room with Reuben. Mum was a nurse. She worked hard doing double shifts through the night. This meant that I spent many a day alone. We had no house help, so I had to fix my own breakfast, prepare meals, clean the house, and do the laundry. Clearly, life in America was different, much harder!

Thank God for twenty-four-hour television. I watched cartoons, comedies, soap operas, movies, and got a thorough introduction to American pop culture by watching sitcoms like *The Jeffersons, Three's Company, Different Strokes,* and *Happy Days.*

Mum quickly opened up about her past. She told me about our agonising separation in England, and her subsequent misunderstandings with my father and his side of the family. I felt like I was caught in a wake of a past she could not reconcile. Sometimes, it was as if I was the personification of her unspoken frustrations. It was as if she had finally found someone with whom she could vent her frustrations.

The problem is, I had also been involuntarily victimised by her broken history. I had spent most of my childhood without my mother. I loved those people—the people who had stepped up to raise me. They were the only family I had, especially since she wasn't there. They had modeled love, care and family to me. They had taught me values, manners, and character. They had taught me how to be a strong woman. They were my family. Her denigration of them, however justified, caused me some emotional confusion and considerable inner turmoil. I had to deal with it. I could not blame my mother but refused to allow her feelings to discolour my perspective of Dad and his family.

As months rolled on, we discovered more about each other and with each passing day, I began to appreciate my new home.

I was in New York, one of the world's greatest cities. The world-famous Empire State Building, which I always dreamt of visiting, was only a few minutes' drive away. I had previously learnt all about New York in a geography class in Uganda. Being one of the cultural hubs in the world, New York also hosted big sports and concert events. None thrilled me like the big Jackson 5 concert at Garden City in 1982. It was to be their final joint concert. The Jacksons were iconic even in Uganda. Everyone knew Michael Jackson. I was stoked. I had to go see them. I remember pleading with Mum to take me. She couldn't, but one of my aunties, Susan Musoke did. I was in awe—the great Michael Jackson was right there. I had a good seat, so I took it all in. Oh, and I got my souvenir jersey shirt and posters too. I still have my Jackson 5 keepsakes stowed away safely.

It was time to write my friends about my adventure. I missed them. I missed familiar. I missed normal. I missed our jokes, our games, our food. I missed Uganda. I couldn't wait to tell them about this new country, America. The size of buildings, cars, schools, stores, even people. Everything seemed big here.

'I was sad when I heard that she was leaving for the USA. She promised to keep in touch, and she did with letters, postcards, photographs, we knew everything about her'!
—Robinah Mukasa (Friend)

# MANHATTAN

We lived on Roosevelt Island—a charming little island located between Manhattan and Long Island. Roosevelt Island is a narrow island in New York City's East River. It is about 2 miles (3.2 km) long, and lies between Manhattan Island to its west, and Queens on Long Island to its east.

Though small, Roosevelt Island has a distinguished architectural history. It was developed as a middle-class neighbourhood from the ruins of prisons and hospitals and has always offered nice riverside walks without crowds and unobstructed views to Manhattan's Upper East Side. Though very close to the city, it was quiet and peaceful.

When the first apartments opened in 1975, my mum and Dad Maxwell were some of the first residents there. The Island's development is mostly clustered along Main Street. Our address was 555 Island House, Main Street, Apartment 1502, on the fifteenth floor.

Mum and Dad Maxwell worked in Manhattan, and although I could clearly see Manhattan through my bedroom window, I had never been there.

One morning, several days after my arrival, Mum said, 'Today you're coming with me to the city'. I was thrilled. On Main Street, we hopped on to a red bus. Few stops out and the driver announces: 'Last stop'. I wondered why; we hadn't left the Island. Anyway, I followed Mum out of the bus through a turnstile where she inserted coins for me and her. We walked into what looked like a huge red metallic cubical looking box. 'Are we still going to Manhattan'? I asked Mum. 'Yes'! she replied, but didn't explain.

I waited anxiously, not sure how this thing was going to move or which direction it was going to go. It had no front or back. I didn't see a driver either. There were no wheels, no foot breaks, and absolutely no tires to move it. Passengers strolled in one by one. Some sat but most stood up and held on to the straps hanging from the roof of this thing. I sat on one of the few seats and waited.

The door closed. 'Welcome to the Roosevelt Island Tram, please hold on', announced the man standing near a small dashboard with a set of red, orange and green buttons.

'Tram'? I muttered. 'Yes, it's a car…a cable car', Mum whispered. Suddenly, the tram pulled up along the wired cable… oooh woooh…I almost screamed. My mother giggled. I tried to look around to see if anybody else was amused. No one seemed to be bothered. *We must be safe,* I thought. So up and down the East River we went. On the other side was a similar cable car moving in the opposite direction. A great adventure indeed! Within a few minutes we descended and approached our stop. This was my first time to set foot on Manhattan.

The tram was to become my daily mode of transportation to and from the study centre where Mum had enroled me in preparation for my college entrance exams.

My mum was heavily pregnant with Monique, but like most New Yorkers, she was a fast walker. I struggled to catch up to her.

Here I was on this Island that we had read about in geography class in Primary school. I was fascinated by the huge, tall buildings—and there was the Empire State building in front of me. Was I dreaming? I couldn't stop looking up. 'Stop staring like a villager', cautioned Mum. 'Now that you are New Yorker, you should start acting like one'.

At the time, the only people I knew in New York were my mum and her family. I used to write letters to my friends back home. I missed Uganda. I longed to be in the company of other Ugandans, but for months, I didn't see anyone else.

As I said, mum was a registered nurse who worked day and night shifts at the local hospital. I only saw her briefly between shifts. She had no time to entertain guests or to socialise.

My stepdad Maxwell, on the other hand, was very social. His Ghanaian friends, Tony and Lawrence, came by from time to time. Dad Maxwell was a fun-loving person. His favourite three things were Roosevelt Island, African food and good music. He would cook for us Ghanaian food. I was introduced to fufu, kenkey and many other dishes. When he wasn't at work, he would stand by his music player for hours shuffling albums of Nigerian highlife music by Fela Kuti. He'd play his all-time favourite song 'Sailing' by Christopher Cross. He'd put on record after record, and joyfully danced. My brother 'Son Rueben' (as Dad called him) would later mimic his father. By 4 years of age, Rueben had become a little African DJ who knew all the Ghanaian highlife music.

Life in America was fast. Everyone seemed so busy and driven. Rarely did I see my two aunties, my mother's sisters, Susan and Lillian, who had come to the USA before me. The isolation was daunting. I had to get with it, this culture.

But first, it was time to get serious with school.

Prior to admission into college, I had to study for three major exams: the Scholastic Aptitude Test (SAT), General Test (GRE) and Test of English as a Foreign Language (TOEFL). My mom enrolled me into a study programme that would help prepare me. From the study centre, I would go to the New York Public Library on 5th Avenue. I readily frequented the library. It is there that I met Zaida Bentacourt, my first real friend in America.

Zaida was from Venezuela. She and I would study together. Since we both loved Burger King, we had lunch there together and often hung out at her house in the Bronx. We went to the movies, met each other's families and really bonded. I really felt at home with her.

'I was elated when she moved to New York. It felt like I had a daughter on the East Coast. She would come over to Dallas during the holidays, and I would some-times visit her in New York. Whenever my mom came to visit, she'd bring stacks of chocolate to take back to her "sisters" in Uganda. One thing about her is this: Sylvia always had a big heart'.

—Cate Bamundaga (Aunt)

## BACK TO SCHOOL

In January 1983, Mum enroled me at City University of New York at La Guardia Community College in a liberal arts programme. I was able to complete the two-year associate degree within one year.

I applied to study journalism and public relations at New York University (NYU). Thankfully, I was accepted and was awarded an academic scholarship for my bachelor's programme. To cover my other academic load, I applied for grants and a student loan.

In the middle of my programme at LaGuardia College, I moved from my mother's place at Roosevelt Island to live with Auntie Susan Musoke on 135th West 24th Street Room 101.

The house, notably called Jean D'Arc (akin to Joan of Arc), was neat and quaint. It was owned and operated by Catholic nuns. Aunt Susan and I shared a room. Eventually, she moved out and I took it over. I was finally independent.

> 'Even after she moved out on her own, I so looked forward to going over to her place. We would watch TV, do dinners and special outings. Sylvia always seemed to have it together. She was even keeled and comfortingly calm. Even when we did conflict, she was always civil and composed. She always had this aura around her'.
>
> —Reuben Codjoe (Brother)

> 'As long as I can remember, she was always around. Even after she moved out, I'd spend the funnest weekends with her. Yes, Sylvia is funny. She dutifully attended my dance recitals; yes, my cool big sister was always there. She is someone I always looked up to. She modelled confidence for me, encouraging me to always speak up. She is also huge on family and culture. In fact, it is her dedication to the Ugandan community that helped spark my interest in Africa'.
>
> —Monique Codjoe (Sister)

With rent, bills, and upkeep, I needed to get a job.

A dear friend, Namata Katongole, whom I had met at a Ugandan function at the United Nations, helped introduce me to a local telemarketing company. Granted it wasn't great money, it was better than nothing. I enjoyed getting a paycheck.

> 'I met Veronica and Sylvia around the same time, we became great friends. We would attend functions and

parties in and around New York City. We looked out for each other. I remember helping her get a telemarketing job at a local call centre. We were everyday New Yorkers; riding buses and trains like everyone else'.

—Namata Katongole (Friend)

Before I graduated from LaGuardia College, I procured an internship at *W Magazine*, a women's wear daily. That was huge for me. There I was, working with reporters and editors. Granted I was not being paid for this, but I loved the behind-the-scenes buzz of the fashion industry in one of the world's largest cities. Yeah, I really could do this. I enjoyed telling stories and used every opportunity to share my own journey as an African emigrant. Maybe journalism was my cup of tea after all!

As soon as my admission to NYU was complete, I decided it was time to pursue this childhood dream of doing journalism.

'Initially, I didn't approve of her major. I felt like journalism didn't offer much to her as a black woman. I wanted her to do law or nursing. She wouldn't budge. She obviously saw something I didn't'.

—Rebecca Musoke (Mother)

I loved school. My favourite professor, Richard Hall, inspired me most of all. He made African history fun, even though I was an African. He had a pretty good handle on the subject and had in fact written extensively about it. In that same class, I met Jennifer Gordon who would become a very good friend.

There was another professor who didn't like me much. I think he was racially prejudiced. He also taught African studies, but had a habit of making things up. One day he claimed that the reason Africans liked bending so much is because we love being close to the ground. Which I knew was wrong and so I decided to correct him which didn't go well with him.

A new chapter in my life was unfolding. Although it was much slower than I wanted, I could see a small, but bright light ahead. I continued to hope that God would open doors for me in this great land.

Excited as I was about the US, I missed Uganda. *Five years,* I thought. *Sylvia, that's all you need to finish school and get trained for success.* I had promised myself to only spend five years in America.

'Regardless of the distance, she stayed in touch; "You should come study here in the USA", she said one day. Almost right away, she had found me a school, and processed all my entry requirements. After all that effort, I changed my mind, and you would think she would never talk to me again. Not Sylvia. She continued caring for me like nothing had ever happened, never taking it personally and always thinking the best for me'.
—Elsie Mukasa-Kalebu (Friend)

## 'YOU HAVE NO BUSINESS HERE'

We had been given an assignment in my editing class to work on a story that talked about the Purple Heart, a prestigious medal awarded to war heroes. Everyone else knew what that was, except me. When one of my professors saw my work, he spoke piercing words that really stuck with me: 'Sylvia, you are from Uganda, right? You don't even know what a Purple Heart is? How do you expect to make it here in journalism? Look, you need to know about America. That is going to be your primary audience. You Africans, you do things very differently. Listen to your accent. You even speak differently. I suggest you consider another major. You really have no business in Journalism'!

I don't think he was being mean or racist. He simply spoke from his narrow experience. Notwithstanding, his criticism reinforced a negative voice that I had been fighting.

I have this vivid memory of me reading the news to my paternal great grandma Jajja Sarah Namyenya. I'd mimic Eva Mpagi, Uganda's then-top female news anchor, in my version of the evening news.

Prior to my enrolment at NYU, I had taken elocution classes at a local radio station, despite my mum's objections. The instructors were dismissive of my prospects in the news business because of my 'different' or 'thick' accent. They said people would not understand me because I didn't sound American. The only reason they didn't kick me out is because I was paying them.

Right after that experience, I did something completely counterintuitive. I decided to look for a job reading news at a local radio station, NBS Radio. I was eager to prove my professors wrong. They hired me. I'd get up early in the morning to read the six o'clock news. Even then, I was constantly criticised for not pronouncing words correctly. Besides my accent, I had studied 'English-style English', which is not always the same as American English. That was before major broadcasters like CNN recruited reporters with different accents.

Shortly thereafter, I heard about an England-based gospel music group from Uganda, Limit X. When I heard their music, I was blown away. *Can Ugandans really sing like this?* I wondered. They sounded like Boyz II Men, the top R&B group at the time. They blew away any other African group that I had heard in America or anywhere else. I had to find them and interview them for our station. I thought my audience would love it.

I spoke to my programme director who immediately agreed. I was excited. We called Limit X and aired their story on our show. This is when I met Dennis Sempebwa, the group leader at the time. Little did we both know that twenty-seven years later, he would help me write and publish this story. Small ecosphere, right?

Gradually, I started to concede. Maybe they were right. Maybe my accent was getting in the way of hitting the pinnacle of achievement in this industry. Maybe it was time to shift to something else.

I decided to make a shift into public relations.

# chapter 7

# SSITEREDDE
## (Unsettled)

While heading to class one day, I stopped by a registration desk manned by a vivacious Ghanaian girl. She was shouting, 'FEED THE CHILDREN OF SOMALIA. THEY ARE STARVING'!

Her desk was covered with sad images of emaciated kids with blotted bellies. I was stunned... observers were dubbing it the 'Great African Famine'. It was 1984. How could that be? I would have never imagined that there was an African country that couldn't feed its people, let alone its children. My heart was tugged. I wanted to hear more. She invited me to join the African Students Association, seeing that I was indeed an African. I wholeheartedly accepted. Even though NYU was the largest private university at the time, there was only a handful of African students. That small community would become like family to me.

The African Students Association NYU also introduced me to student activism against apartheid, a brutal South African government policy that enforced racial segregation and discrimination. I remember proudly wearing my badge and adorning my FREE NELSON MANDELA t-shirt on subways. We participated in NYU anti-apartheid sit-ins and protested against American companies who were doing business with the South African government.

## UGANDA FOCUS

During my early days in the US, I was hoping that I would meet Ugandans through Auntie Susan and Lillian, but never did until the fall of 1983 when I connected with Namata Katongole at a United Nations function. Namata's family had been in the US since the early 1970s. Her parents were kind-hearted and humble. I enjoyed conversations with her dad who had just retired from the United Nations. She had five brothers and sisters whom I got to know, especially Namusisi, or Sissy. Namata and I became inseparable at parties and other functions. She still remains one of my closest friends.

Later that year, I started to get involved with the small community of Ugandans from in and around New York.

We would simply get together or meet on ceremonial occasions such as birthdays, weddings, anniversaries, which were typically hosted by popular Ugandan families in New York including the Mubandas, Ngobis, Musokes and Mugwanyas. We started to organise events and get-togethers at the Uganda

House, where the Ugandan embassy is situated close to the United Nations headquarters. This led to the formation of the Uganda Cultural Society.

> 'We were both very active in the Uganda Cultural Society. Our goal was to outreach to Ugandans far and near via our quarterly newsletter. We'd meet to write articles and synergise ways to enhance our core message of culture, interconnectedness, and community. Sylvia was both extremely efficient and dependable. She was also genuinely interested in our history as a people, and a nation. She wished she had had more exposure. "If I had only spent more time in Kampala", she'd lament'.
>
> —Mary Weeks Kironde (Friend)

We organised New York cultural evenings which became very popular, especially among Ugandans on the East Coast. Fashion shows depicting traditional wear were an instant draw. But still, I felt we could do more as a community. We started hosting events to engage Ugandans from all across the American Diaspora (South, West Coast, Northwest and even Canada) to New York.

> 'I had gone to see Veronica Kalema and a couple of friends in New York when Sylvia and I met. They were the cool kids in town who knew exactly where to hang out'.
>
> —Barbara Mulwana Kulubya (Friend)

The vision was to gather Ugandans to share and find solutions to the different challenges we faced, to celebrate our rich history and cultures, and to entertain ourselves. The response was phenomenal—Ugandans eagerly replied to invitations to get together as Ugandans in the US.

'I met Sylvia at Uganda House in New York in the summer of 1987. I had just moved from London with my father, Joshua Wanume Kibedi, who had been appointed Permanent Representative of Uganda to the United Nations. As a teenager, I was thrilled to be embraced in the community by Sylvia and her aunt Lydia Sebugwawo. We quickly became good friends. We were young, in a bustling city full of opportunities. Still, we endeavoured to stay connected to our roots in Uganda, and we looked out for each other. I particularly remember the tram ride to Roosevelt Island on weekends—always a delight! Maama Rebecca and Mr Codjoe always warmly welcomed Sylvia's friends… absolutely enjoyed spending time with little Monique and Rueben. What fun times. What beautiful memories'!

'Uganda House was home to the permanent mission of Uganda to the UN. We'd converge on the 10th floor, our meeting point and venue for many cultural and social events. Sylvia was very active in organising these community events'.

—Lydia Kibedi (Friend)

All this opened my eyes to another need: information dissemination. We needed a tool—in addition to word-of-mouth—to help us notify people about the important happenings within our community. We needed a platform to showcase our continuing story as Ugandans living in New York/New Jersey. I came up with the concept of a community newsletter which was supported by Mrs Mary Weeks and Mr Michael Muganga. Together with David Wapenyi as the layout and design desktop artist, we published a newsletter called *Uganda Focus!* It gave us a place to connect and get to know each other as one big family. It was the first such forum for communication among Ugandans in the USA and Canada. During the same period, the Uganda North American Association of New York and New Jersey was formed. The Association held cultural evenings and a multitude of events which attracted Ugandans from other states.

Through the newsletter, other communities across the country learnt about what we were doing in New York and New Jersey. Before long, cities such as Washington and Atlanta jumped onboard. Ugandans across America started to get excited about the concept of having culture and community gatherings. Consequently, the Uganda North America Association (UNAA) was birthed in Atlanta, Georgia, in 1988 with 200 members. Thirty-two years later, UNAA is still going strong with more than 120,000 members.

'She was a very young, active member of the Ugandan cultural community in New York, and as a journalist, the one who *initiated* a Ugandan community newsletter, which had 1,500 subscribers throughout the USA. This newsletter advised various Ugandan communities in the US about effective ways of organising annual cultural events. It was the amalgamation of these individual cultural events in various cities in the US that gave birth to the now powerful Uganda North American Association or UNAA'.

—Jean Sembeguya Matovu (Friend)

# TURMOIL AT HOME

From the time I left in March 1981 to December 1985, news from Uganda was not encouraging at all. The nation was still in turmoil. Political unrest, numerous military coups—utter chaos!

> 'After a disputed election brought Milton Obote to power again in Uganda in 1980, one of his opponents, Yoweri Museveni, led an armed resistance against the government. The subsequent Ugandan "Bush War" between Museveni's National Resistance Army (NRA) and the government's Uganda National Liberation Army (UNLA) lasted from 1981 to 1986. In 1983, ethnic tensions began to fracture the UNLA. President Obote, an ethnic Lango, was accused of favouritism at the expense of the Acholi, who mostly comprised the officer corps. After confronting Obote with these and other complaints, General Tito Okello staged a coup d'état with the help of a group of Acholi. Okello ousted Obote and installed himself as president on July 27, 1985. Okello was ousted himself by Museveni and the NRA six months later'.[1]
>
> —Irvin D. Coker (USAID Mission Director)

It is interesting to note that during the rebellion in the mid-80s, the young heir-to-the-throne of our abolished Kingdom

---

1. *Association for Diplomatic Studies & Training*: "The Overthrow of President Obote and Evacuation from Uganda", July 21, 2014: https://adst.org/2014/07/the-overthrow-of-president-obote-and-evacuation-from-uganda; accessed 12 December 2022,

of Buganda, Prince Ronald Mutebi, secretly met with influential Baganda in various parishes, asking them to support the rebellion. They did. And without their support, the resistance movement wouldn't have been able to find sanctuary from government military pressure within the Buganda region where they were fighting.

On January 20, 1986, Yoweri Museveni was sworn in as Uganda's new president. Jubilation filled the streets as hope for economic and political recovery seemed to return to the country once again.

## THE UNITED NATIONS

Meanwhile, in the very same month, I graduated with my Bachelor of Arts degree in journalism. Initially, Mum wasn't coming to the ceremony. Funny thing is, she honestly didn't think she needed to. She was more focused on hosting my graduation party. I implored her, and thankfully she changed her mind. We were joined by my friends Namata Katongole, Hannington Rwabazaire, Veronica Kalema and her mother Mrs Rhoda Kalema. Veronica was graduating from Princeton University around the same time. In fact, we scuttled out to Princeton for Veronica's graduation ceremony a few days after mine.

'We were both graduating students. Gone were the days of obscurity back in Uganda where we first met as kids. We were grown, independent young ladies now with big dreams ahead of us. We'd hang out over the

weekends; go shopping, sightseeing, partying, club-
bing, travelling, and doing family. I remember watching
her plan the first Uganda culture show in New York.
The idea would morph into what is now Uganda's
premier cultural convention in North America. We
would eventually complete our academic journeys. I
still remember attending each other's graduation ceremonies. Precious memories'.
                    –Dr Veronica Nakibule Kalema (Friend)

A week later, friends joined me to celebrate the milestone. I
couldn't wait to jump into the job market.

I sent resumes and job applications all over the place. I was
invited for a few job interviews including one at the New York
Stock Exchange, but nothing materialised until I spoke to my
friend Grace Edward who encouraged me to apply for a job at
the United Nations Department of Public Information where
she was working. 'But I speak only one language, English. The
UN requires at least two', I complained. 'Don't forget your
mother tongue Luganda, that's your other language', Grace
insisted. I honestly didn't think knowing Luganda would help,
but I was wrong. I applied and got the job as a public information assistant, also known as a United Nations Tour Guide.

I loved it. It was as though I was being paid to sit in a perpetual classroom. My international, multilingual team members
included Africans, North and South Americans, Europeans,
Australians, and Asians. It was an amazing place to work. We
had to know everything about the sprawling facility—the Security Council, the General Assembly, and so on. But way beyond
that, we had to be well schooled in the history of the United

Nations and its global operations. We would get daily updates on political hotspots such as Palestine, the Gaza Strip, and all the critical United Nations humanitarian efforts around the world. Reason being, we had to be able to answer any question posed by our esteemed guests. Did I say that I absolutely loved my job? Well, yes, I really did!

'While in Uganda, her relatives lived in the house opposite ours. My sisters and I would hang out with them. When I met Sylvia in New York, we quickly bonded. We worked together at the United Nations headquarters in New York. We were assistants in the Department of Public Information. We absolutely loved it: the daily briefings, the curious guests, the ambiance—the buzz of working at such a huge global organisation. We got to meet lots of people. I still remember her poise, even her posture. Yes, Sylvia was totally bred for diplomacy. While some might have become overwhelmed by it all, we ate it up. In fact, we both wanted more! It is this insatiable appetite for current affairs that really bonded us all the more... Hard as it was to juggle work with grad school and family, we still found time to have fun'.

—Grace Edward Kabuye (Friend)

## IS THIS OUR TEACHER?

United Nations offered me great opportunities. I could have worked there longer; I felt like I had the perfect job which was totally suited to my personality. But much as I enjoyed my job, I decided to pursue a goal I had been nursing for a while—complete my master's degree. I figured I needed to do it, or I would never get to it.

I immediately enroled in a master's programme with the New York Institute of Technology in 1990. I was accepted on a fellowship which allowed me to teach and work alongside the dean while I pursued my degree. My tuition was waived, and I was given a stipend that helped cover my bills while advancing my experience and education.

When the lift (elevator) opened, there stood this strikingly beautiful young girl who smiled at me. Her name was Judy. We exchanged pleasantries. She said she had seen me in the dean's office, and promised to pass by the office to see me.

'I remember the student introductions on the first day of class. I thought, *Hmm…she is from Africa. How cool.* I was intrigued, being from Haiti myself. Ethnically, we were undoubtedly linked. Furthermore, interests seemed to align. Apparently she felt the same way about me, so we built a friendship. We really liked to hang out. We made friends together. We even visited each other's houses. She would invite me to the annual Ugandan convention. Sylvia became my Ugandan sister, and I her Haitian sister'!

–Judith Walker (Friend)

I was assigned to teach public relations and the history of communication. I still remember my first day in class. The students gasped when I walked into the classroom. 'Is this our teacher'? I must have looked so young and inexperi-enced. Some of the girls were rolling their eyes at me. I was so nervous; but thanks to the school dean, Dr Felisa Kaplan, I hung in there. She once told me, 'Look Sylvia, I have no doubt you can do this. You know your stuff, plus your work at the UN has more than prepared you. Just ignore them and keep going'. Her words encouraged me. I decided to tough it out—teaching and developing myself while completing my master's programme.

As much as I enjoyed the unfolding story of my life in America, I longed to return home to Uganda. There was an agitation inside me. Although I had mastered my way around New York and the parallel intricacies of the American culture, I still felt foreign. I was an alien, which unsettled me.

## FAREWELL JEAN D'ARC

Jean D'Arc in Manhattan at 253 West 24th Street had a strict visitor policy that completely restricted all visitors regardless of relation. I mean, not even my sister was allowed to visit my room 101. Everyone had to stay in the downstairs lounge.

Well one day I decided to invite Veronica up to my room. I basically snuck her up, but one of the nuns found out. At the crack of dawn, one of the other nuns came up to my room and was completely outraged. 'How can you do this to us, Sylvia'? she asked. 'I am so sorry, sister. I am terribly sorry. I will not do it again', I pleaded. 'No way. You must leave', she barked.

Thankfully, she showed compassion towards me and forgave my transgression. I would stay at Jean D'Arc for seven years.

I remember, while still at Jean D'Arc, when I got my driver's licence, I was so excited. I rented a black Chevrolet Sundance, and together with my friends Namata, Lydia Kibedi and Aunt Lydia Sebugwawo, we drove to the Atlantic City resort in New Jersey, a two-and-a-half-hour drive for a first-time driver. I always wondered how they allowed an inexperienced girl to drive them almost 200 kilometres.

'When Sylvia got her driver's licence, she was extremely happy, and to celebrate she rented a black car and drove us to Atlantic City! She had taken her driving lessons within the city, and this was her first time on a superhighway. We were so young and naive, but she was extremely confident and we sat in the back seat of the car as passengers, totally oblivious to what dangers could possibly happen'!

–Lydia Kibedi (Friend)

By the grace of God, we made it there and back, with the exception of a 'little ding' into a car ahead of us, and that was just because I was busy juggling cassette players in slow traffic. Thank God the elderly couple in the white sedan let us off with only a fuss and a yell.

From Jean D'Arc, I moved to Upper Manhattan and into Yorkville Towers at 1623 Third Avenue on 91st Street. It felt good to have my own autonomous living space with my own bathroom and most importantly, independence.

Apartment 3A was a spacious, modern and beautiful three-bedroom apartment which had been leased to my step-dad Maxwell; and since he wasn't using it, he let me occupy it. But since I couldn't afford the rent by myself, I decided to get roommates to help out.

I took the master suite and was more or less the permanent resident.

'I first met Sylvia at the United Nations language training department where I had gone to improve my English. She was working on her French. We hit it off in the corridor by the notice board where I was scanning advertisements for rentals. When I mentioned to her that I was looking for a place to stay she quickly said that she was looking for a roommate. My mum had warned me not to trust strangers in New York City, but somehow, I made an exception for Sylvia. As soon as I saw the place, I accepted the offer, and moved in with Sylvia and Woody and enjoyed some of the best times of my life. They were two beautiful people'.

–Virginie Mongonou (Friend)

Initially, I shared the apartment with Miguel Arranz from Venezuela and Hector Martignon from Argentina. Hector moved out and Laura Coleman, an African American, moved in. When Laura left, in came Widmark Valme (aka Woody) from Haiti.

'I approached Miguel Arranz about the possibility of moving into their apartment as they were looking for a roommate. Miguel invited me to dinner at the house. Unfortunately, I got so drunk that night that Sylvia asked, "Miguel, is this the person you want to bring into our apartment?" So she turned me down. Thankfully, he convinced her that I wasn't so bad after all. Almost immediately, I could see that she was a person of high integrity. Eventually, we became friends. She met my Haitian family, and in turn introduced me to the Ugandan community in New York where I made many friends who still call me Mukasa, the Ugandan name Sylvia gave me. Before I physically visited Uganda, I had attended the Ugandan American Convention in New Jersey'.

—Widmark Valme aka Woody (Friend)

Miguel soon left and Virginie Mongonou from Central Africa Republic moved in.

It was a great cultural experience. We bragged about having the best coffee and traditional cuisine. Our apartment was a great attraction for dinners and parties—its size, central location and beauty attracted the young people our age.

'Sylvia was classy, yet also humble and kind. She was of excellent conduct, a good example for a young black woman to gals like me coming to New York City from Paris. She would spend hours in her bedroom watching news, and yet also found time to socialise with us. Whenever I cooked and invited my Francophone friends, she would happily join us. We'd eat French food and dance to Zouk music which she loved.

She wanted to practise her French with me, while I was also eager to practise my English'.

—Virginie Mongonou (Friend)

My different roommates would host friends who enjoyed their traditional cuisine. Miguel in particular was fond of cooking, and he loved to experiment with new foods. Woody introduced us to Haitian music while my love for Zouk music stemmed from Virginie's Africa Francophone roots.

'I still remember hanging out at Zanzibar Restaurant and Club one night. A popular Zouk tune was playing. Suddenly, Sylvia hits the dance floor. We were stunned as she glided on the floor to the French-Caribbean beat. I had found a dance teacher. Again, seeds that would later lead to the launch of her own ballet and dance studio in Uganda years later'.

—Debra Rutiba (Friend)

'1623 Third Avenue where Sylvia lived was an upscale apartment and a place where we made some wonderful memories. To us, it was simply grand! It was a superb meeting point for many of Sylvia's friends. Her room-mates were from different continents—Africa, the Caribbean, Asia and South America. With her UN connections, I had the opportunity to meet all kinds of people from all around the world'!

—Lydia Kibedi (Friend)

I completed my master's degree and graduated with honours in 1991. My thesis was on communication for development with emphasis on Africa. I felt that instead of running away from my unique roots, I would embrace them and use that as a pivot for my academic journey. As part of my final work, I produced a public service announcement, which actually won an award.

When news got back to Uganda, the national television network eagerly aired my public service announcement in recognition of outstanding achievement on behalf of our nation.

I felt like my time at the United Nations was not done yet, so I took another job there in the audio section of broadcasting which afforded me an opportunity to attend numerous high profile international meetings in all the main chambers of the United Nations—the General Assembly, Security Council, Trusteeship Council and the Economic and Social Council. Later, I transferred to the research department of the United Nations Center for Transnational Corporations, where I worked as a research consultant in developing a publication on the world's largest transnational banks.

As I look back at this transformative season of my journey, it is without a doubt that the favour of the Lord was upon me. Some of it might seem like coincidence and happenstance, but as someone who has always trusted God, I strongly believe that it is He who opens and closes doors. I can clearly see that God was gently guiding me throughout my time in America.

'We used to talk a lot about work and career development; always looking for ways of advancing ourselves. Together with another friend named Zane Nobbs, Sylvia and I started a consulting firm called UNISM Inc. I have never mentioned this to her, but I always looked up to Sylvia. I still do. She was different, had her head above her shoulders; and even though somewhat reserved, always approachable and easy to talk to. I would bounce ideas off her. We would discuss and exchange information. We had so many good laughs. I remember her asking me one day after a squash game, "Woody, what are you doing with your life?" The question left me thinking for long after that moment. Without a doubt, she was a good person to have in my life'.

—Widmark Valme aka Woody (Friend)

chapter 8

# SSEEKAKASA
## (Uncertain)

### THE BAGANDA

A brief history about the Baganda…

The Baganda culture is very unique and rich. His Majesty, the Kabaka once said, 'A good number of tourists come to East Africa to tour animals, but rarely does one come across such rich history, proper organisation, wonderful culture, and highly civilised customs as we have in the Buganda Kingdom'.

Baganda acquired civilisation many centuries ago. We engaged in music, dance, drama, poetry and several performing arts. We had our own traditional instruments, folk songs and indigenous cultural expressions.

Our arts and crafts were exquisite. Our women weaved amazing baskets, mats, beads, pots, crafts, handbags, and handmade jewellery. Our men made clay pottery and created an indigenous fabric from the bark of a *mutumba* tree called bark cloth. It is just recently that the rest of the world is starting to pay attention to the ingenuity and dexterity of this amazing fabric.

Buganda has beliefs, traditions and values that are deeply rooted in our culture. This explains the propagation of social harmony, tolerance and overall discipline. We created proverbs and idioms to preserve our rich culture and to equip our people with the critical life skills needed to do conflict, fatherhood, marriage, old age and so much more.

Many of our elders were centennials who lived remarkably healthy lives. Traditionally, all food was eaten fresh and never fried. Our staple food is mashed green bananas, which we steam in banana leaves. We like cooking our vegetable or meat sauces in *luwombo* or specially prepared banana leaves over woodfires. We love bananas. In fact, we even make beverages from certain species of bananas.

When the European explorers came to the Buganda Kingdom in the 19th century, they were shocked at the advancement of our people. The English Prime Minister Sir Winston Churchill was so supremely impressed by our heritage and culture that he named the country, Uganda, the Pearl of Africa.

The British would subsequently use the Baganda to administer their colony throughout the territory. Our indigenous language—Luganda—spread to all parts of the country. Our cultural norms were quickly adopted by other regions and tribes. Today, more than 85 percent of the Ugandan population understands Luganda.

My first trip back home to Uganda was in the summer of 1986. The nation was still in chaos. However the prospect of permanently returning to Uganda was still high on my list—I couldn't extinguish the fire inside. I made short trips home in 1988, and 1991. I knew deep down in my heart that I would one day return for good, but just didn't know when. I loved my country and wanted to be part of Uganda's next chapter.

'When she returned to visit from the USA, she looked me up, and we took trips looking for all our acquaintances. She wanted to check up on our old circle of friends. Even after life scattered us all over the world, Sylvia always made it a point to look us up and keep in touch'.

—Robinah Mukasa (Friend)

## TESTING THE WATERS

'A casual chat that started when she came to the office to see my former boss, the late James Mulwana, made for the beginnings of a friendship that would span over three decades. I found Lady Sylvia to have such a great personality—she smiled, was warm, outgoing, and very easy to talk to. We realised we had a lot in common, hit it off from the get-go and have been lifelong friends ever since'.

—Joyce Kisubi-Muyanja (Friend)

I first met both Mr James and Mrs Sarah Mulwana in 1987 at my friend Barbara's graduation at Northwestern University in Chicago. I was also a friend of their daughter Primrose, and eventually Geoffrey their bother. Over the years, we became very close. Through our conversations, Mr Mulwana noticed that I was very keen to return home to work, which sparked his interest. He wanted to help me figure out how. He was a great man. I looked up to him as a father and a mentor. I would bounce ideas off him, and he was always willing to listen and ready to advise.

In 1990, he had invited me to attend a business conference with the theme: Attracting American Investors to Uganda, at the John D. Rockefeller Estates in Pocantico Hills, Westchester County, New York. It was organised by Maureen Reagan and sponsored by the Rockefeller Foundation.

As I started to really struggle with my options, I thought about Mr Mulwana. I knew he would be a real resource for sound advice, so I called him to share my ideas. He was encouraging. He proposed, 'Why don't you come try it out and test the waters first? Come and help me coordinate our annual Uganda Manufacturers Association event'.

I was excited at the prospect. I thought, *Look Sylvia, you are not making some huge, impulsive leap into a totally new field with no direction. You are going to go spy the land first, so why not?* Since my contract at the UN was up for renewal, the timing seemed right to explore options for a possible return to Uganda.

Meanwhile, I was also getting tired of New York's fast life, even though I was somewhat addicted to it. I had even considered moving out of the city to another state, but I just couldn't wrap my mind around doing life at a slower pace anywhere else.

In July 1993, I boarded a British Airways flight with final destination to Entebbe, Uganda. My resolution: If I could find a plausible path to return to meaningfully contribute to the country in the next six months, I would seriously consider a permanent move.

'Our friendship grew even stronger when we eventually had the opportunity to work together at the Uganda Manufacturers Association trade fair in the early 1990s. She lent her expertise to marketing and promoting the event throughout the region. We drove around town in a red Toyota chasing down printers for catalogues and banners, trying to beat deadlines and putting everything together. It was during this time that I realised what a hardworking, principled, dependable, and tenacious person she was. Getting the job done promptly, efficiently and effectively was her middle name. Yet she was very respectful to everyone she engaged with'.

—Joyce Kisubi-Muyanja (Friend)

Mr James Mulwana impressed on me to work for the Uganda Manufacturers Association (UMA) as a consultant for what would be Uganda's first major international trade fair.

I hit the ground running, doing what I did best—public relations.

I produced a magazine for the show which put me right in the throes of logistics and production for the show itself. It was a resounding success!

My friend Barbara Mulwana was also in town. She had relocated back to Uganda after working for Good Year, the tyre manufacturer headquartered in Ohio, USA.

'Sylvia called to tell me how she wanted to check out the possibility of a relocation back home. She wasn't sure about her reentry after such a long time away. There was a lot going on developmentally. The economy was bustling. Seemed like a good time to be back. My dad, who loved her dearly, hired her to do public relations for him. We had lots of fun. Being together helped her realise that a return back home was doable; that she could survive after all'.

–Barbara Mulwana Kulubya (Friend)

During the consultancy period at UMA, I stayed at the Mulwana's residence. It so happened that Mr Mulwana was involved in organising the coronation of King Ronald Mutebi, the son of Sir Edward Fredrick Walugembe Mutesa II, the 35th Kabaka of Buganda and first president of Uganda, who had been exiled in England following the desecration of the Kingdom. He had been pronounced heir to his late father in 1969 and performed the traditional rites at his funeral in 1971.

Just then, my mind raced back to an interesting conversation I had with an old friend, Dr William Kalema, earlier in 1991. He had approached me with an interesting proposition: 'Sylvia, there is somebody I would like you to meet'.

'Who is this'? I questioned.

'Well, he is a prince. He lives in London'.

'Does he have a name'? I quipped.

'Prince Ronnie Mutebi'.

'Are you kidding me'? I replied emphatically.

Reluctantly however, I agreed to check out the proposition, although my mind had great reservations about it. I was 29 years and no ties yet, so I suppose I didn't have anything to lose by keeping the opportunity open—just in case.

William happened to be Prince Ronnie's good friend. He really believed I was the girl for the prince, so he refused to accept my reluctant response.

A couple of weeks later, he called back. 'You should come and meet the prince in Uganda', he said excitedly. 'I will fly you here. Meanwhile, please send some pictures for him to see you'!

'I don't like the idea', I replied. 'And NO...I am not sending any photographs to anyone', I quipped. Honestly, I really didn't think that sending photos of me for that purpose to him, or anyone else for that matter, was appropriate.

Several months later, my aunt Joyce Sebugwawo was visiting New York and the topic somehow came up. 'We are looking for a suitable wife for the Crown Prince', she revealed. She then added, 'We should take you to see him. You'd be perfect. You'd make a good queen. You should give me one of your nice pictures to show him'.

It was an interesting coincidence because my aunt and William hadn't discussed this.

'As a matter of fact, someone else has told me about this', I replied. 'But I just don't think so. That is not me'!

While I am certain that such a proposal would thrill most young women in my position, particularly Baganda women, I was reluctant about the whole idea. I was aware of my body clock. I knew it was time to settle down and start a family, but not like that. Besides I wasn't so impressed by some of the stories that I heard about Buganda royalty. History is replete with unflattering stories about royal families in general around the world.

'A few of us who knew him felt tasked with the responsibility to find him a suitable mate. The search was not easy because he was very particular. Even though we identified a few potential candidates, our efforts did not bear any real fruit. Sylvia's name wasn't one of those that I brought forward for Kabaka's attention because she was in America and our focus was on girls around Kampala; however, I did mention it to her privately when I saw her in New York. She didn't take me seriously'.

—Owek (or honorable) Joyce Sebugwawo (Aunt)

## GOT NOTICED

The Mulwanas invited me to hop along with them to Naggalabi for the coronation ceremony. Taata and Maama were also planning to attend and were super excited, in fact, I remember running into them as we climbed the hill to attend the ceremony. There was mass jubilation across the country, particularly throughout Buganda.

There was a sea of people, literally hundreds of thousands. We had to park a good distance away from the main grounds.

Fortunately, my hosts were notable dignitaries with special seating privileges, so I was able to enjoy the auspicious ceremony up-close. That 31st day of July 1993, King Mutebi was officially installed in a glowing coronation ceremony.

A few days later, there was a private dinner party hosted by Mr Gordon Wavamunno in honour of the Kabaka's coronation. Only fifty guests were invited, and among them were the Mulwanas. Barbara couldn't leave me behind and the parents were more than happy to have me tag along, so I joined them.

Mr Wavamunno is a business mogul and a close friend of the royal family. He has an exquisite mansion in Muyonyo overlooking Lake Victoria. Before moving inside for dinner, we chatted over cocktails in the garden. Just then, we were told that His Majesty King Ronald Mutebi had arrived. We formed a greeting tunnel with men on one side and women on the other. Down came the Kabaka greeting his guests as he made his way into the house. Women were either curtseying or kneeling as he approached. He shook hands with everyone in the line. He said hello to me in the same manner as he did with everybody else, rather uneventfully; not that I was expecting anything different.

I would later learn that the King had actually noticed me that night. In fact, he sent a note to our mutual friend William Kalema with these words, 'Oh, I saw Sylvia last night'.

Soon after the coronation, it seems, the Kabaka had a series of invitations for other private functions, and one other such event was hosted by his longtime friend Betty Kajubi. I had friends among the Ssenteza Kajubi family whom I had known for a while back in the United States. So, I received an invitation from them to an even more intimate barbeque get-together at Betty's place in Mpererwe.

Tom Kajubi offered to pick me up, and on the way we stopped by the Kabaka's residence in Kololo; after exchanging pleasantries, we joined his convoy and headed out to Betty's residence in Mpererwe.

Aside from the occasional glance across the room, we really didn't have much more interaction that evening. I could feel his intrigue, my mind wondered as the night wore on.

Early the following morning, my friend William reached out to me. He had received another note from the Kabaka: 'I saw Sylvia last night at Betty's place, but we couldn't talk'!

I was charmed, and excited. *I think he likes me. I think he really likes me,* I thought.

William would eventually pass on my number to him. Over the next few months, we spoke several times.

## I AM NOT READY

'When I first heard about her desire to move back to Uganda, I was nervous. But then I remembered how connected she was. She had a large family back home, not to mention an influential grandfather who loved her to bits'.

—Namata Katongole (Friend)

It had been six months since I returned home. 'So, Sylvia, are you going back, or are you staying'? quizzed Mr Mulwana. 'No sir, I am not staying. I am going back to New York', I responded.

'Why'? he pondered. 'Look, you've done a very good job with our trade fair, the exhibition, and the magazine. You are remarkable. There are plenty of opportunities for you here in Uganda. You should reconsider'.

I was quiet. He was right. But I had been pondering this decision for months. Granted my six months in Uganda had been blessed with good success, and clearly my skills and training were needed in Uganda, but I just wasn't ready for the question, much less its implications.

'I am not mentally ready to stay in Uganda', I quipped. He was quiet. His countenance showed clear disapproval and disappointment.

I vividly remember my last conversations with the Kabaka after he learnt about my imminent return home to New York.

'So you're going back to the US'?

'Yes I am'.

'When are you going to visit Uganda again'?

'I am not sure when, but I feel that it is better for me to return to the United States for now'.

To be perfectly honest, I couldn't see any open doors to effectively serve my nation with my training at the time.

That was in January 1994.

As I boarded my flight back to the USA, I knew that a new season was upon me. I was watching the clock. Five years in America had turned into thirteen. New York was getting a bit old for me, much as I loved the city with all its hustle and bustle. I needed to move. It was time to make a move out of New York.

That spring of 1994, I packed my bags and relocated to Silver Spring, Maryland.

Mum couldn't understand why I was walking away from all those opportunities in New York to start afresh in a whole new city without a job. She truly believed that I belonged in New York. I remember her saying, 'Sylvia, if you can't make it in New York, you can't make it anywhere'. I said, 'No, Mum, the correct saying is, "If you can make it in New York, you can make it anywhere"'!

# chapter 9

# NSAZEEWO
## (Resolved)

I moved in with my cousin Ann-Loi Nagawa Kyewalabye and her family for about a month. Eventually, I would move into my own place in Georgian Towers at 8715 First Avenue, Apartment 916 D, (and later 920 C) in Silver Spring, Maryland, where I lived for the next five years.

My life in Maryland was quieter.

I had to quickly get back into the job market, so I took on temporary consulting work. My first assignment was a communications job with the insurance giant, BlueCross BlueShield. Shortly after that, I accepted another consulting job with the Federal National Mortgage Association, commonly known as the mortgage giant Fannie Mae.

'When I got a job with the World Bank in Washington DC, Sylvia had already moved in the area. She recommended that I get an apartment in Georgian

Towers in Silver Springs, Maryland—the same building where she lived'.

—Virginie Mongonou (Friend)

As much as I didn't want to get isolated, it took me a while to warm up to the Ugandan social circuit in the area. In fact, I really never connected with anyone deeply other than Ann-Loi, her husband Sam and, later Michael Kyompi Sebalu and Ruth Kirindi who were my room mates at some point. I felt like I had entered a different phase of my life. I didn't have the energy to reach out and do the relationship dance like I had done in New York.

I was technically not a New Yorker anymore, although New Yorkers like to say that 'Once a New Yorker, always a New Yorker'. In fact, my friends refused to accept my new 'statehood'. Even when I helped organise the Washington DC UNA event, they still introduced me as Sylvia from New York, thanks to the thirteen-year history.

'I have known Sylvia for more than 30 years, and at the time I met her in New York, we were both young professionals. Then we moved to Maryland, and there began a season filled with adventure and life discoveries. It's not every day that you make an instant connection which makes for a lifelong friend. Although we talked about pretty much anything—husbands, kids—we mostly discussed the plight of Africa and Uganda in particular. Friday nights at Boukom Café, a favourite African restaurant in Washington DC, found us talking about how we could impact our homeland. Little did we know that we were planting seeds in preparation for what God had planned for her'.

—Debra Rutiba (Friend)

After about a year, I took on more permanent work with Gardiner, Kamya & Associates Accounting firm. Among other assignments, I worked on a World Bank project that took me to Uganda in 1997. I also coordinated a joint venture project with Maximus, a Virginia-based management and administration service company.

'In June 1994, I told a good friend of mine, Sam Kyewalabye, that our Washington DC firm, Gardiner, Kamya & Associates, PC (GKA), was looking for someone to work in our professional development department. He said he had "a very bright and hardworking Ugandan lady" in mind. I asked her to connect us. The next day, Sylvia called. She was professional, truthful, and seemed eager to work. Before I hired her, I cautioned, "Sylvia, there is no free lunch here," as I did with every recruit. She hit the ground running. With over 200 professionals and high-profile clients like the US Federal Government and other state governments, international organisations (including the World Bank, Inter-American Development Bank, etc.), she had a full plate with non-stop, overlapping deadlines. She held her own. Eventually, she would become a fully integrated member of the firm's management. By late 1997, Sylvia had transferred to our firm's management consulting group. She was assisted by Bonita Witherspoon, who later became one of her dear friends. She was particularly interested in health issues faced by developing countries. Since we had a healthcare contract funded by the World Bank that required on-site work to be done in Uganda, she insisted on joining the delegation to Uganda'.

—John Mukalazi Kamya (Former Employer, Friend)

# I SAID, 'YES'

The Kabaka and I stayed in touch a few more times in 1994 after I returned to America, but the long-distance dynamic soon took its toll. We lost touch. I later heard that he was dating someone else. I honestly didn't feel slighted or passed over. I genuinely wished the best for him. Besides, deep down I really wasn't sure if we were suitable for each other.

One spring day in 1998, Anne-Loi's husband, Sam Kyewalabye, also a cousin to the Kabaka, called me to say, 'Ronnie is looking for your number, should I give it to him'? I tried to probe as to why but he just laughed and said, *'Ndowooza kubuzaako'* meaning 'Maybe just to say hello'. I said 'yes', although I later learnt that he had already passed it on to the Kabaka. As a Muganda, he couldn't decline the King's request. In fact, he didn't need my permission to give him my number.

He called almost right away. He was quick to say that he was passing through Washington, DC, and thought he should call to say hello. It had been four years since we last spoke. We had a cordial chat, and although we didn't meet, a slow, curious fire was kindled.

He would call me again shortly thereafter while he was in London. We enjoyed our conversations. It seems as though we were both ready to get serious with whatever was going on between us.

Over the next few months, we would email back and forth. With every interaction, excitement was building. We decided it was time to meet again, so he flew me out to London to meet with him.

At the time, he, the Kabaka, was without a doubt Uganda's most eligible bachelor. He was also arguably, the most fascinating single man, so any fraternisation with a woman was juicy tabloid material back in Uganda. Meeting in the UK seemed safer and allowed us to get to know one another outside of the public eye.

I honestly never thought about the ramifications of our budding love affair. And in my simple mind, I was in love with Ronnie, not the King of the great ancient Kingdom of Buganda. At 35 years old, I was ready to settle down, get married and start a family.

Confidants started talking to me about royalty, and what marrying the King of Buganda really meant. Mum, who didn't like the idea, tried to caution me about a potentially turbulent entry into the monarchy. I listened, but never really took it in—on purpose. I was preparing to marry a man, and not his status. Had I fully comprehended the magnitude of our union, I would have been totally freaked out. In hindsight, they were fully justified to caution me. Indeed, I was naive and overly simplistic with the incredible responsibility that the King's wife—the Nnaabagereka—carries.

One evening, an email popped into my inbox. It was Ronnie. The body of the email was rather disarming. It said something like: 'Dear, Sylvia, I think I am ready if you are.' *What? Is this a proposal?* Yes, it was. Ronnie was asking to marry me…by email? Definitely not the ideal proposal that this girl had waited for all her life. Perhaps a bit un-romantic? Oh well. I don't really remember everything I wrote back, but I said, 'YES'!

'I have been friends with the Kabaka since the 1960s. I knew Sylvia Nagginda long before they got married. When I saw her at the coronation of the Kabaka Mutebi at Buddo, she had grown into a very beautiful, polished young lady. Soon after the coronation, His Majesty Kabaka Mutebi started going to various conventions in the USA; and after some time, it was announced that he was going to marry Sylvia Nagginda. I got involved in the preparation for her wedding. I had the honour of organising a Kasiki for her in London, which was a "sold-out" event'.

—Jean Sembeguya Matovu (Friend)

'When I heard that he had proposed to her, I thought, Wow...the Kabaka has got himself a good one. He is lucky to have her! Sylvia is a straight shooter. When she loves you, it is for life! You can always count on her commitment and undaunted dedication'.

—Harriet Kagwa (Friend)

'In late 1998, I received news that the Kabaka was going to marry Sylvia! For me and the rest of the GKA staff, it was a mind-blowing surprise. So, I called my friend Princess Mazzi to see if she knew anything. Well, she laughed and reminded me of a rather mysterious delegation I had hosted a few months back. She revealed that their mission was to conduct due diligence on Sylvia on behalf of the King and the Kingdom of Buganda. I was of course excited for her. There was an unfolding, real-life fairytale happening right in front of me and everyone at GKA. Bonita organised a major celebration with over 500 guests

at the World Bank Auditorium for the Ugandan community in the Washington DC Metropolitan area'.
—John Mukalazi Kamya (Former Employer, Friend)

## JUST A SPECTATOR

When I shared the news with friends and family, reactions were mixed.

'"Reuben, I am going back to Uganda!" What? Uganda? I was shocked and a bit hurt when Sylvia told me this. I thought, *Why would you leave the US and move back to Uganda? Who does that?* She just kept saying, "It's time Reuben. This is my time to do this"! I could see that look, and I knew that this was much deeper than a mere tryst. She was determined, although I could also see the uncertainty in her eyes. She was nervous. So I said, "Whatever will make you happy sis, you go for it"'!
—Reuben Codjoe (Brother)

I remember breaking the news to some of my friends:

'I also still remember the first time she broke the news of her affair with the king. I had gone to visit with her and she couldn't hide the glow on her face as she broke the news to me'.
—Debra Rutiba (Friend)

Mum, on the other hand, was more cautious. For years, she had been pushing me to get married. And now, here she was all apprehensive: *'Ebyekimbejja bino...ha naye onobisobola'?* meaning, 'Royalty is no small thing, Sylvia...are you sure about this'? She had major reservations about the marriage; and if she could, she would have stopped me from going on with it. She took long to warm up to the idea.

> 'It was common knowledge that the king was looking for a bride. When I heard that he was interested in Sylvia, I thought it was just a fling. Besides, I was sure that the Sylvia I knew was too classy to be bogged down in a palace to play some noble role. Much to my surprise, turns out that the king was serious. He really wanted to marry Sylvia. And she was going along with it. Seemed I was mistaken about my daughter'.
> —Rebecca Musoke (Mother)

> 'When she first told me, I thought, *What? Him...the Kabaka likes you?* I was not sure she was cut out for it. Remember, we were the emancipated women who were protagonists of women's rights. How on earth was she going to play this really traditional role of Nnaabagereka'?
> —Barbara Mulwana Kulubya (Friend)

As the weeks wore on, Ronnie proposed that I should come to visit Uganda, so we could move the ball forward. We were past emails and phone calls.

> 'When I heard that Sylvia was getting married, my first question was, "Is this a forced marriage?" But then I thought she's too smart for that. A queen in a traditional institution? I thought it didn't suit Sylvia. She's so independent for that. I called up our mutual

friend Furaha Bishota who assured me that Sylvia wasn't being forced, and that this was her choice'.

—Virginie Mongonou (Friend)

'I had mixed feelings of happiness and anxiety. I feared for her venturing into the unknown—and at the same time I was sad to think that I was about to lose a friend. It was a really painful time for me! Uganda was too far from the USA. I was going to miss the closeness we had. Ironically, I was also excited because then again, I thought, she was getting married to the King. Let her go'!

—Ann-Loi Nangendo Fulu (Aunt)

Travelling back to Uganda was no small feat for me. My job with Maximus allowed me no vacation time to spare. Regardless, I had to go figure out what my next step was going to be. I had to go! So, I requested Friday and Monday off from work. My boss agreed. Soon after work that Thursday afternoon, I drove straight to the airport and boarded my British Airways flight to London, onward to Entebbe.

Aunt Joyce and Uncle Dan Sebugwawo picked me up and took me straight to their home in Mengo.

In the evening, Ronnie treated me to dinner at an Ethiopian restaurant in Kansanga, where he laid out my packed weekend schedule.

On Saturday, I was formerly introduced to Ronnie's sisters—Dorothy Nassolo, Sarah Kagere, Alice Zalwango, and Diana Teyegala—at Banda. They were kind and gracious to me, although clearly, understandably apprehensive. They were checking me out. I could almost feel their piercing eyes. Their gazes seemed to say, 'Who is this girl'?

On Sunday, February 14, 1999, my delegation—Dad, Taata, Aunt Sarah, Aunt Kolya, Uncle Dan—and I dressed up in *busuutis* and *kanzus*, our traditional formal wear, and drove out to Banda. When we arrived, Katikiro Ssemwogerere and a few other Buganda officials were already seated in the garden. We joined them.

After the pleasantries, the Kabaka announced: *'Tufunye Nnaabagereka'*, (meaning 'I have found a wife') to the *Katikiro* (or Prime Minister) of the Buganda.

With that said, there was rapturous applause and a few speeches. It was done. How surreal! The day flew by as precipitously and fleetingly as it all came together. By Sunday night, I was officially engaged to be married to King Ronald Mutebi.

'To be honest, I thought that her marriage to His Majesty would mess up my friendship with a very special person. Incidentally, my brother David Segawa, a friend to the Kabaka, called me with excitement. *"Kiwede,"* he remarked, meaning, "It is done!" He was excited for his friend, the king! Funny that we were both close to them'.

—Elsie Mukasa-Kalebu (Friend)

'Sylvia is the oldest grandchild in the family. It never occurred to me or her uncles that she could ever be the Nnaabagereka of Buganda. Yes, this was a huge surprise. Without a doubt, it is God who has delivered such a huge gift to us'.

–Kolya Ekiriya (Aunt)

My relatives went into a frenzy. They had a wedding to plan.

'I was on the wedding organising committee. Everything was huge! I was shocked by the public interest. Everyone wanted to be involved. We met for days, planning what would ultimately become the wedding of the century'.

–Fred Lutalo (Cousin)

On Sunday late afternoon, I was taken straight to the airport to catch my flight back to Maryland. As I sat back to try and rest in flight, I marveled at the happenings of the whirlwind weekend, I could not put my finger on any predominant emotions. Was I happy, relieved, excited? Not sure. I was numb.

'Sylvia rang and told me that she would be in Uganda during Valentine's Day weekend, but that I needed to keep my lips sealed about the upcoming trip. I said, "Of course, you know you can count on my discretion". At the back of my mind, I'm thinking, *Hmmm, could it be what I think this is?* Lady Sylvia can be cautious and is known to keep things close to the vest, a trait we appreciate in each other. So I knew not to press for any further details. I believe it was a Friday evening when she arrived in Uganda. She told me she was staying at her aunt's house and would keep in touch. On Sunday evening, she gave me details on the chronology of events that had happened at Banda during the weekend, as she headed to the airport to catch her flight back to Washington, DC. I was ecstatic. There was so much to digest, so many questions, like would she keep her job? The phone calls were endless, and the mood was one of joy, excitement, and enthusiasm all over the Kingdom after word of the engagement had gotten around'.

—Joyce Kisubi-Muyanja (Friend)

All the pomp and circumstance, the ceremonial festivities, the newspaper reports, the television specials, completely over-whelmed me. Was it really me? Everything was much, much bigger than I ever imagined. It really felt like all this was hap-pening to someone else, and I was just a spectator. It almost didn't feel real. Perhaps it was my coping mechanism kicking in to protect me from the shock. I felt like if I had allowed myself to get swept up into the enormity of it all, I would be emotionally stressed.

'When I heard about her betrothal to the king, I was not concerned at all. I knew she'd make the perfect Nnaabagereka. Her grandfather and great grandfather were chiefs to the Kabaka. Her grandmother was a chief's daughter. She was surrounded by some of the finest Baganda women anywhere in the Kingdom, who taught her manners, poise, royal etiquette, and high society. She also learnt plain hard work and grit. It is no surprise that Sylvia is not your regular, stay-com-fortable-in-your-palace queen. Whether she knew it or not, she was groomed for this'.

—Dr Veronica Nakibule Kalema (Friend)

On Tuesday morning, I was back at work.

I tried to explain to my boss what had just happened, but it was all foreign to her. 'I am going to marry the King of Buganda'. You can imagine her bewilderment. 'What? You? How? What does that even mean'? She wanted to make sure I wasn't making it up, so she googled the Kabaka, me, and Buganda. You should have seen the look on her face. She was happy, then terrified for me. It seemed as though everyone who knew me had the same expression—fear.

> 'As soon as the news broke, the frenzy began. Everyone wanted to know about her. And then there were the skeptics, cynics, and haters. But hurtful as it was to hear the gossip, we focused on the wedding plans. As we inched closer to the big day, it hit me. Much as I was happy for her, my friend was leaving—for good! No more spontaneous visits; no more impromptu calls and long conversations. It was sad'.
>
> —Debra Rutiba (Friend)

## FAREWELL AMERICA!

As news of the engagement spread throughout the Ugandan community, curiosity heightened to fever pitch. Ugandans from the USA, Europe and all over the country were wondering, *Who is this girl? Where did she come from? And how is it all happening so fast?*

> 'While people in Uganda were dealing with the media frenzy, in Maryland we were busy planning how the

soon-to-be-Nnaabagereka was going to transit from the USA to Uganda'.

—Ann-Loi Nangendo Fulu (Aunt)

Debra Rutiba, Anne-Loi and others organised a bridal shower for me. Friends and well-wishers came. Once again, it felt surreal—the whole thing felt totally unreal. In some ways, it was as if I was watching someone else's life.

'I had seen my father and brother John hurriedly dash out dressed in *kanzus*. Hours later, they returned visibly jubilant. "We have been officially introduced to the King", they gleefully said. "What"? I quizzed. "Yeah, Sylvia is to marry the Kabaka"! Needless to say we were shocked, and ecstatic. Almost immediately, the farm was mobbed by paparazzi. They wanted to know everything from what food she ate, where she played, and where she slept. It was all over the news. We were tightlipped which drove them crazy. So, they started inventing stories about her. They claimed she had four kids. Others said she had been married before. We ignored it all and decided to focus on the wedding'!

—Eva Nassejje (Aunt)

In June 1999, our families organised the traditional introduction ceremony called *Kwanjula*. *Kwanjula* literally means 'to introduce'. During this ceremony, the future bride formally introduces her future husband and closest circle to her parents, relatives and friends. It is a very big deal in our culture. In fact, these ceremonies are as weighty as the actual traditional marriage ceremonies.

'You never heard any funny stories about Sylvia. She was the perfect girl. So, when we heard that the Kabaka wanted to marry her, we were elated and confident he had chosen well. Next thing I remember was hosting the *katikiro* (or prime minister), princes, princesses and dignitaries from all over the Kingdom. They had come to officially ask for her hand in marriage. We could not contain the crowds. We thought the whole district came out to the *kwanjula*. Their king had found a wife—our daughter'.

—Mummy Edith Luswata (Stepmom)

The *kwanjula* takes place at the home of the future bride's father. The father receives the guests who include the future husband, his sisters, brothers and other close relatives. The future husband's parents normally don't come to this occasion. It's supposed to be a private function where the bride through her official *ssenga* (one of the father's sisters) introduces the groom to her immediate family members who typically include the parents, siblings, maternal and paternal aunts, and grandparents.

Being out of the country all the way back in Maryland, I hosted the ceremony in absentia. My official *ssenga* was Aunt Sarah Kamya-Kiyingi. The Kabaka's delegation was received at my father's house in Nkumba. My dad had long moved from Kololo to live in Nkumba not far from my grandparent's place where I grew up. Later on, during the pre-wedding festivities Aunt Cate Bamundaga also featured as ssenga. In essence, I had two official ssengas.

Traditionally, the Kabaka does not attend his introduction, he is represented by the kingdom prime minister. Owek. Joseph Mulwanyamuli Ssemwogerere officiated on his behalf.

'When the plan was concretised, I prepared for the kwanjula. You know the Kabaka doesn't go for okwanjula, it is the katikiro who goes. We were just a few people; about twelve. After that, I announced in the Lukiiko (the Buganda parliament) that the Kabaka had finally given us a Nnaabageraka'.

–J.G. Mulwanyammuli Ssemwogerere
(Katikiro/Prime Minister Buganda Kingdom 1994-2005)

I truly wished I was there to see it all. Instead, I was thousands of miles away alone in my apartment in Silver Spring trying to imagine what was happening back home. Social media wasn't a thing then, so I had to wait for calls from my friends Barbara Mulwana and Joyce Kisubi to update me. They did a good job getting news to me. My family on the ground also kept me abreast of the goings on. After the function, they sent me a video which captured the entire occasion in real time.

As the days rolled on, it became clearer and clearer that life as I knew it was about to completely change.

In June 1999, I submitted my resignation notice at Maximus Consulting. I still remember the tearful farewell lunch with my team.

'I'll never forget when I first heard the news. She didn't really tell me about their relationship until after the engagement. *Wait...the king has a thing for my sister? Was she moving into a palace?* I didn't know where to go with it. I knew her life was about to change big time. I had a thousand questions but knew that I couldn't ask them all'.

–Reuben Codjoe (Brother)

I started packing up after eighteen years of my life in America. I spent several days at it, giving away most of my stuff, selling a few and shipping the rest to Kampala.

I sold my maroon Toyota Rav4. It was the first and only car I had ever owned. I had purchased it brand-new just a few years before. I had learnt how to drive while in New York, but since I lived and worked in the city, owning a car didn't make financial sense. I had a beautiful sofa set which I sold to a friend, Petulla Alleyene—and more than twenty-two years later she tells me that she still has it—in excellent condition.

On June 1, 1999, the Kingdom of Buganda made an official announcement of the upcoming royal nuptials. The *New Vision* newspaper article read: 'Kabaka Ronald Muwenda Mutebi's wedding to Sylvia Nagginda Luswata Ssebugwawo is confirmed for Friday August 27 at the Lubiri Palace'.

The emotions of impending change were heavy. I had to focus on the next chapter. But first, I had a wedding to plan.

## A WEDDING TO PLAN

I needed a wedding gown. Yes, every girl's dream, and this girl wanted nothing but the absolute best. I wanted a conservative gown that mirrored a *busuuti* or *gomesi*, our *kiganda* traditional wear. I wanted something unique—a convergence of culture and convention. I received proposals for a design from three vetted designers: Beatrice Iga, Beatrice Babirye and Sylvia Owori.

All were good, but I could only go with one, so I selected Beatrice Iga's design. I loved her style and creativity. She is a highly experienced, US-trained designer of haute couture, couture, and ready-to-wear fashion, who had won a number of awards in designing. Her designs were sold in upscale American stores.

> 'I didn't like the rush, but never mind my opinions. Who wouldn't want to make the gown for the king's bride? And indeed, she was inundated with inquiries. Given the time crunch, I really wanted to assist Sylvia and so I recommended my friend Beatrice Iga'.
> —Cate Bamundaga (Ssenga)

After packing and shipping off my belongings, I flew to Dallas, Texas, to be near Beatrice while she made the gown and bridesmaids' dresses. With so little time to pull it all together, I needed a face-to-face sit down through the entire process.

> 'Sylvia was clear on the concept of her gown—she wanted a traditional *gomesi* combined with Western style. I made a few sketches of wedding gowns for her to choose from. After she saw them and interviewed me, we had a long discussion on design and fabric until she finally settled for one'.
> —Beatrice Iga Musisi (Friend)

We immediately started shopping for fabric, for both my gown and all the bridesmaids' dresses. For weeks, Beatrice styled, cut, re-cut and produced the most gorgeous wedding gown, and bridesmaids' dresses completely from scratch. She had an extra bedroom, so she insisted I move in with her.

'Sylvia, we have some serious work to do here. I need you here 24/7', she announced.

> 'Nnaabagereka's wedding gown was a *kiganda gomesi* (also known as *busuuti*-inspired gown) made of ivory silk taffeta, with the boned-fitted bodice decorated with golden embroidery with natural pearls. The fitted boned bodice was designed with a square neckline with two big buttons, big sleeves to replicate the real traditional Baganda *gomesi*. The sleeves were elongated to change the look of the shorter version of sleeves on the traditional *gomesi* to a modern *gomesi*, now called "Nagginda Style" (named after her). The petal sleeves, full skirt, and the twenty-foot silk tulle veil train was inspired by Western wedding gowns. Martha Lewis, an American shoe designer, designed the shoes to match the bodice of the royal gown. I also designed the bridesmaids' and flower girls' dresses. The bridesmaids wore gold to complement the bride's ivory silk taffeta wedding dress'.
>
> –Beatrice Iga Musisi (Friend)

Beatrice and her husband, Patrick, were so gracious to me during my stay with them. I have to mention that Beatrice did all this while facing serious personal hardships. Their son was fighting cancer. She would work on the gown in the car while parked in the hospital parking lot during his chemotherapy treatments. Words cannot express my gratitude to her. I am forever in her debt.

> 'Unfortunately, soon after I had agreed to make the royal wedding dress, my son was diagnosed with very

aggressive cancer. However, I couldn't get out of the commitment. I prayed to God for guidance and wisdom, strength and courage to design and create the royal gown. Sylvia was kind, respectful and easy to work with. I thought to myself, *Indeed, she was the right wife for the Kabaka'*.

—Beatrice Iga Musisi (Friend)

Meanwhile, Uganda was buzzing with news of the royal wedding. The media was in a frenzy about it.

Two weeks prior to the big day, on August 15, 1999, I bid my friends and family farewell to head back home to start a completely new life in Uganda.

Ugandans in the Dallas-Fort Worth, Texas, area gave me a big sendoff. Aunt Cate, Uncles Abraham, Eddie, Shemmie with other relatives organised the function, together with Mr Senkayi, Mr Turyamureeba and other friends in the area.

I boarded my British Airways flight to Entebbe. I was booked in business class. An upgrade from my usual travel in economy. *Not bad,!* I thought. My rather large hand luggage—the wedding gown—was handled with extreme care.

No, it wasn't five years in America as I had anticipated, but a long eighteen years of extremely hard work, formal education, on-the-job training, lots of pressure, plenty of growth, great world exposure and wonderful experiences. Clearly, that season was over.

'When I learnt that she was going to be queen, I honestly did not know whether to be happy or not. She is kind and loving, but extremely private. My heart almost grieved for her. Such a public platform would undoubtedly cause unwanted attention. How was my Sylvia going to handle this? How was she going to do her favourite fun things like movies and dancing? Who had persuaded my friend to enter such a public space?'

—Lydia Nakatude Sserebe (Friend)

'When I heard that Sylvia was going to become the Nnaabagereka of Buganda, I simply couldn't believe it. *I know her!*, I told myself, *This is big!* I was enchanted and genuinely excited for her. I called every member of my family to announce the news. On the wedding day, I was glued to the television, I didn't miss a thing. There she was, all tall, so beautiful, elegant, and calm in this gorgeous wedding dress and a crown. *This role is for her*, I thought, *her calling*'.

—Norah Rwakihembo (Friend)

'At GKA and in Washington, DC, those of us who knew Sylvia remember a warm, confident, hardworking and meticulous professional. Everyone is proud of her and will always be'.

—John Mukalazi Kamya (Former Employer, Friend)

SECTION 3

# OKUGEREKA N'OBUWEREZA
(Service)

'Kewerimidde Kakira Mbegeraako'
(Luganda Proverb)

Translation:
*'Better To Grow It Yourself Than Beg For It'*

# chapter 10

# OKUDDA AWAKA
## (Homecoming)

When I finally landed in Entebbe, I walked into a completely new life. The VIP treatment right from the airplane gate was disarming. I didn't need to fill out immigration forms or landing cards, let alone carry my own passport. In fact, I didn't even see my luggage or ever think about it. I had bodyguards as part of my official security detail which ensured safe passage through the press pool, paparazzi and hundreds of adoring fans and well-wishers, to the cars parked outside the VIP entrance of the airport.

'Everything happened so fast. I was clueless. Next thing I hear is "Sylvia is coming, but we need to sneak her into the country without people knowing". Being a security officer at the International Airport, I thought, *Easy, I will process her documents and get her in through the VIP lounge without anyone knowing.* Nope. Before she even landed, the press was on to us. Even after she was cleared, there were cars filled with journalists tailing us all the way to the gate of the house in Nkumba'.

—Fred Lutalo (Cousin)

# THE ARRIVAL

A police motorcade whisked us straight to my father's home at Nkumba, where the eager press was already awaiting our arrival. I was told that some of the paparazzi had jumped over the front gate and stormed into the front room. It was crazy!

Questions were swirling through my mind: *Do I really need a police escort with bodyguards? Why is the press so curious? Is this going to be my new life?*

I wondered what my friends and family thought.

'When I first heard the news of her betrothal to the king, I was pleasantly surprised, but not entirely. After the news sunk in, I could see the writing on the wall. Even in childhood, Sylvia was not like any of us. She was exceptionally put together, tidy, polished, and deeply perspicacious. She was always clearheaded and firm. Our grandparents were particularly strict with her, almost too strict in fact. They were insistent that she mastered key habits and disciplines that are critical to leadership. Completely unbeknownst to them, the Sebugwawos were raising a queen, the next Nnaabagereka of Buganda'.

—Robinah Nakamate Kyazze (Aunt)

The plan was to stay with Dad for a few days. He seemed distressed by the wedding plans, the daunting logistics, and the media frenzy. The press had literally camped outside his gate. They didn't want to miss any opportunity to photograph or interview me. I had no privacy. So I moved, like I had planned.

Barbara had offered her home to me. It was convenient, private, and most importantly, unknown to the press, so no paparazzi. I moved in—Plot 20 on Kyadondo Road in Nakasero.

'I wasn't in Uganda at the time, but I was more than happy to have her crash at my house. Giving back to her in this way was the least I could do. She had been so good to me over the years. I could imagine that she would need time away from the public eye. Little did I know just how much'.

—Barbara Mulwana Kulubya (Friend)

My family had identified my aunt Juliet Nabwami, my father's cousin, to be my lady-in-waiting. She moved in with me in Barbara's place and later at the palace. She had been well briefed about her impending duties, as were Mama Jasi Kyendibaza and the royal cook, Mubinge Namudu, who were also to move in with us to Kireka Palace.

Barbara's family constantly checked up on me to make sure I was doing well. Suddenly, I was hit with a severe cold and a fever. With the wedding fast approaching, I needed immediate treatment, so Mr Mulwana brought a doctor to the house to treat me. I was miserable, weak, and anxious.

Since the bridal and bridesmaids' outfits and accessories were all in order, I needed to attend to selecting a hair stylist and makeup artist. Thankfully, my relatives had identified some, who needed to be vetted by me. My friend Namata, who had come to attend the wedding, also moved in with me. Additionally, I had the help of a fulltime assistant assigned to me by the palace.

'I was so honoured to be a part of her celebration. It was a total madhouse, but what a moment! I was happy to serve her in any way that she needed me to. It was a thrill seeing literally millions of people excited for my friend's wedding to the Kabaka'.
—Namata Katongole (Friend)

During the two weeks leading up to the wedding, I barely saw my future husband, except for a couple of days, and of course during counselling. Yes, we had to participate in a six-week (two hours each week) pre-marital counselling track as a requirement of the Anglican Church. But given the special circumstances, we were fast-tracked. For four days (four to five hours each day), we attended multiple individual and couples' counselling intensives with key Namirembe Cathedral clergy, including Bishop Balagade Sekaade, Primate of the Church of Uganda.

One evening, Ronnie sent his driver, Haji Sendikwanawa, to deliver a package to me. Haji knelt as he handed me the package which contained a post card and a book titled, *Men are from Mars; Women are from Venus* by John Gray. The card read, 'Sylvia, I hope you enjoy reading this book. I haven't read it yet, but I am told that it is full of good insights. Love, Ronnie' dated '5:30pm 6/1st/99'. The date on the card was a couple of months back; not sure if it was a mistake or if he had written it before my return for the wedding. Regardless, I thought that was thoughtful, and certainly cute.

# PREAMBLE

Early Friday on August 22, we convoyed out of Nakasero to Taata's farm in Nkumba for the *kasiki*. This is a traditional pre-wedding celebration held at the bride and groom's home the night before a wedding. The closest thing to it in the Western culture is a bachelor's party.

On our way over, we stopped by Dad's house. My dad, Mummy Edith, sisters, brother, and other relatives, including my godmother Mrs Kiwanuka, whom I hadn't seen since primary school, were all waiting for me. The women dressed in *busuutis*, and the men in kanzus, our traditional garbs.

My Maama and Taata were obviously overjoyed. They had been in the company of Kabaka Muteesa in the 1950s and '60s so were familiar with Buganda royalty. So grandfather was always quick to inform everyone around that *'Nze bino nabilaba da'!* meaning, 'I have seen all this before', and he would add that my marriage to the Kabaka wasn't his first encounter with Buganda royalty. 'I took two of my sisters to get married to Mutebi's grandfather, King Daudi Chwa', he declared. Needless to say, he was very excited about the merriment.

I was shocked at the crowd size as we pulled into Jajja's compound. Jubilation filled the air. This was way bigger than I had thought. The festivities included prayers, speeches, traditional dances and plenty of food and drinks.

'I remember the massive pre-wedding ceremonies. Tons of gifts, functions and visits from the royal family, palace officials and the Buganda government.

We were completely overwhelmed by the crowds. We slaughtered nine heifers and prepared truckloads of food to feed everyone, but it wasn't enough'.

—Eva Nassejje (Aunt)

That evening, the city of Kampala was filled with great merriment as had not been seen in years. There were hundreds of bachelor parties across town from well-wishers and extended family members in honour of the Kabaka's wedding.

My bridesmaids were my sister Monique Codjoe, cousins Maureen Kiyingi, Phiona Nagaga, Marian Bamundaga, Sheila Sebugwawo, Kimberly Ibale, Karen Ibale and Kabaka's niece Ndege Simbwa.

'Being in the wedding party, I had this incredible front-row seat to the wedding of the century. Everything was unreal: the grandeur; the paparazzi; the security and the millions of enthusiastic well-wishers who literally shut the city down with jubilation. I got a fresh appreciation for the Kingdom and the esteem the subjects bestowed upon their king and queen. I remember thinking, *Hmmm, maybe I need to find me a prince charming.* It was fascinating to watch her. Her new status had not changed her one bit. She was still the same selfless, disciplinarian, health-conscious sister I have always admired'.

—Monique Codjoe (Sister)

'Sylvia flew out to attend my college graduation, a few months before their grand wedding. That meant a lot to me. Unfortunately, I missed the wedding. This is one of the biggest regrets of my life. How could I'?!

—Reuben Codjoe (Brother)

I drove out to Nkumba the night before the wedding to fulfil the *Kasuze katya* (or 'How was the night?') ceremony which is usually done the morning of the wedding. I walked into my grandparents living room where several grandaunts, grandparents, uncles and aunties were waiting to bid me farewell. For about thirty minutes, I was treated to a most unforgettable ceremony.

Maama, and other notable grandmas and aunties sang ancient songs of gallantry and wisdom to me. I made the rounds with each one of them, literally sitting on their laps and allowing them to offer me their blessing, choice words of wisdom, and tearful farewells, as is our custom. One notable song I remember was *'Okuzaala kujjagana'*, meaning 'Giving birth is a celebration'.

From there, we drove to Dad's house and had dinner as we waited for the Kabaka's entourage for a similar equally important pre-wedding ceremony. This is a ceremonial wedding day ritual in which the groom-to-be picks up his future bride from her father's house, for the last time. In hand, he must have a basket of oil with matches, and a gourd of liquor. Without these items, he cannot be allowed to have his bride.

'When we heard first the news of her engagement to the Kabaka, we were overjoyed. I couldn't think of another person who deserved such an honour. And who can forget the massive pre-wedding ceremonies at her grandfather's place? Never had the Kingdom seen anything like that'!

—Sarah Kamya (Ssenga/Aunt)

At midnight, we journeyed back to Kampala. I was completely wiped out. Rather than jump right into bed, I decided to cross-check my to-do list and make sure that all the outfits and accessories were in order. Consequently, it was not until the wee hours of the morning that I finally stumbled into bed.

## THE ROYAL CEREMONY

On August 29, I woke up feeling extremely fatigued mainly due to lack of sleep and rest. This was my wedding day. Thus, I started preparing myself. From my bedroom suite upstairs, I could hear the downstairs area buzzing with bridesmaids having breakfast and getting ready—hair, makeup, and all.

I had eight bridesmaids including two flower girls, and no maid of honour. Traditionally, the Nnaabagereka cannot have a maid of honour, and neither does the Kabaka have a best man.

Initially I wanted to have only children in the wedding party, but my aunties overruled me, while some of them insisted that their children, my cousins, had to be in the bridal party. After haggling with them to no avail, I gave in. Regardless of my preferences, all the older girls—the entire bridal party selected including my sister—were very dear to me. They were perfect.

I hated the thought of rushing, I wanted to be calm and relaxed as much as possible. So I decided to quietly prepare at my own pace. I locked my door, and powered down my cell phone, which had been buzzing non-stop all morning. I knew that countless well-wishers wanted to personally congratulate me and wish me Godspeed, but I had to shut it all down so I could concentrate on myself.

I was oblivious to how fast the time was moving, until several knocks on my door. When I opened the door, my cousin Maureen Kiyingi, the lead bridesmaid, came in and behind her I heard a man's voice—it was Mr Wasawa Birigwa, who had been assigned as timekeeper.

'*Banange esaawa zigenze tugende*', meaning, 'We have run out of time, let's go'. I told Maureen, 'Please keep him out and don't let him in'. At this time, the stylists were finishing up with my hair and makeup.

> 'I remember the wedding day started early with a drive up to Barbara's house. And there she was—our future queen being made into perfection. I was filled with gratitude to God for this glorious day that He had made. The nation was glued to the television to bear witness to a historic event, a momentous day for my friend'.
> –Debra Rutiba (Friend)

Ronnie and I had planned to touch base before he headed to the church. Well, since my phone was off, he couldn't reach me. Naturally, he decided to just head out, hoping I was on my way.

Big mistake!

By the time his entourage headed toward the church, I was far from ready. I was running late—very late. He rode in a classic Lincoln Town Car stretch limousine. A family friend, Prince Rabbi Sserunjogi Mulondo had specially shipped it in from the USA for the wedding. In fact, it has not been driven again since.

Downstairs, the bridal party was getting restless. The wedding ceremony was being aired live on national television. They could see Namirembe Cathedral, the largest Anglican church in the nation, completely packed. Patrons had started arriving at 5 a.m. that morning, more than six hours early. They could see the Kabaka anxiously waiting for me. Furthermore, our distinguished guests, including His Excellency President Museveni, were also getting restless. Apparently, some thought I had changed my mind, something which I deeply regret to this day. I felt terrible for Ronnie having to sit there and blindly wait for his late-show bride. Honestly, I had no idea that I was that late. Best guess would have been maybe fifteen minutes.

'The King kept adjusting his heavily decorated royal crown. All eyes were on him. Clearly, he was perturbed by the delay. People started whispering, "What if Sylvia has changed her mind? What an embarrassment that would be"! Everyone was wondering the same thing'.

—Eva Nassejje (Aunt)

As news reached me upstairs, I knew we were in trouble. I hurriedly completed my finishing touches and we jumped into our waiting cars.

'The limos stayed in Nkumba overnight, so we wouldn't be late. But a few things went south, right from the get-go. First, Jajja had a near-fatal panic attack on the way to town. Then, Sylvia had this bizarre delay getting to the church, which had the Kabaka, the president, and other important dignitaries waiting for what felt like hours. I knew what everyone was thinking,

*She's changed her mind.* When she finally got there, all was forgotten. She was stunning'.

—Fred Lutalo (Cousin)

Once I got to church, I realised that I didn't have the envelope that Ronnie had given me to hand in during the church ceremony. Good thing he insisted on keeping the rings with him, because I think I would have likely left those behind as well.

'We were totally mobbed. There were people everywhere. By the time we got to the church, everyone was tense. Some rumoured that she had perhaps changed her mind. As I sat there, I was privately pinching myself. I was a nobody—a simple woman about to become the mother to the wife of the King of Buganda. It was mind-blowing'.

—Rebecca Musoke (Mother)

We made it to the church amid rapturous glee. The first thing I heard Dad say to me as he took my arm to walk me down that magnificent church aisle was, *'Mubadde wa'?* meaning, 'Where on earth were you'? I could feel the breadth of my transgression. I had made the king wait; I had made the president wait; and indeed, I had made the nation wait. I felt very sorry indeed!

'I still remember taking her arm to walk her down that aisle. What a relief, especially after that nail-biting wait. Sylvia never told me why she was so late. She just smiled and asked, 'Which side do I stand on'? Words cannot express my pride that day. My daughter was marrying the King of Buganda'.

—John Luswata (Father)

'Nnaabagereka's gown became one of the most iconic wedding dresses of all time in Uganda, often dubbed the most closely guarded secret in the fashion history of the nation, even continent, because so few details were revealed until its debut on the wedding day'.

—Beatrice Iga Musisi, Friend

Did I enjoy the ceremony? Not certain that I did. Everything was so ostentatious, so grand. To make matters worse, I had an irritating cough that I was fighting. I was nervous that I was going to break out into some uncontrollable fit of coughing to the embarrassment of the Crown and our esteemed guests.

'I was at the private party in Kampala where the Kabaka first noticed Sylvia Nagginda Luswata. She instantly rose to prominence upon her engagement years later. Her glamour, activism and determination would make her one of the most influential personalities in Uganda. Being an ex-official, a veteran and an insider in the newly restored Kingdom of Buganda, I was involved in the organisation of the Royal Wedding in 1999, be it at a distance. It was a mammoth affair that brought the Kingdom to a standstill. It was attended by the president of Uganda and kings and princes from all over Uganda and from as far away as KwaZulu in South Africa. Hundreds of thousands of people poured into the Lubiri (the royal palace) in Mengo to see the Kabaka's beautiful bride. As expected, it was a shiny event, but nothing outshone the newly wed Queen Consort's radiant smile.

We were all wowed by it and jubilant that the Kabaka had made such a great choice'.

—The Venerable Archdeacon Emeritus
Prince Daniel Kajumba

I don't even remember much of what Archbishop Mpalanyi Livingstone Nkoyoyo, who officiated at the wedding, shared in his sermon. I unknowingly emotionally detached from what was happening. Days before the wedding, I had overheard Namata's phone conversation with a mutual friend in the US: 'She seems totally indifferent. It is as though everything is just happening around her'. It is days later after I watched the wedding video that I got to see what transpired that day. I enjoyed it; realised that I had actually missed my own wedding. It was indeed a magnificent wedding to say the least.

'I couldn't help but wonder what was going on in her mind. Was she ready for this big role? Or is she just in love? Is she scared? My thoughts were racing as I watched her. She was definitely ready; an admired role model in Buganda; our great intelligent Queen who I am so proud to have known and called friend'.

—Norah Rwakihembo (Friend)

## THE ROYAL RECEPTION

The Kabaka's security detail is composed of Uganda army military soldiers and Baganda security personnel. It includes *abaambowa*, or traditional bodyguards who dress in garbs of bark cloth and *kanzus*. The vehicles have special car licence plates that read, 'Royal Guards'. They led the convoy to Bulange, the palace offices, to allow the masses to travel to the royal palace in Lubiri.

'Then came the big wedding. They didn't want us to be bothered with the pandemonium of the massive reception, so we—my sisters and cousins—only attended the ceremony after which we were taken to an aunt's place and kept there throughout the night. I was bummed out. I knew I was missing the biggest party in town'.

—Prince Junju Kiweewa (Stepson)

I will never forget the drive up to the reception. There was great excitement amid the utter chaos. I was sure the eager crowds were going to overturn the car. They were bouncing it up and down off the ground. We couldn't move because some of them had decided to literally lay prostrate in the streets in honour of their king. They were jubilant, but I was petrified. I was certain someone was going to get run over or fatally hurt.

After what seemed like forever, we did make it to the first reception venue—a VIP luncheon of 5,000 invited guests.

Here, we had the official festivities in accordance to royal protocol. We had approximately two thousand special guests and dignitaries, including King Zwelithini and Queen Tandy of the Zulu tribe of South Africa. There was eating, drinking and enjoying the best of our traditional dance performances.

'I couldn't even see the bridal party, much less see to the end of the large tent which housed the ceremony.

Of course, this was an invitation-only event, but folks made so many fake cards that the place was flooded. The waiters were overwhelmed. There was simply no way to properly serve everyone'.

—Eva Nassejje (Aunt)

We finally made our way to the other side of the palace to kick off the mass reception.

After a few speeches, we were invited to cut the cake. I left my beautiful bouquet behind, and just like that, it went missing—gone, for good. I walked over to the Kabaka and held his hand as we proceeded to cut and serve the cake.

An estimated one million people attended the mass wedding reception. The all-night jubilation was the largest of its kind in recent history.

From the humongous and euphoric reception, our convoy headed to Kireka Palace. The place I now call my home. This would be my third visit to this palace.

The first time was on one of our few dates, way before the wedding and introduction ceremonies. It was a secluded place up on top of a hill, away from prying eyes. It was an ordinary, medium-sized house. We sat on a balcony overlooking the lush green trees and vegetation; in the distance I could see Lake Victoria. It was a beautiful, stunning natural view. We sat and talked for about an hour; I was very chatty with lots of questions. I remember doing most of the talking.

He told me that it was his mother's place which he had inherited. Ronnie's mother Lady Kabejja Sarah Nalule had died of cancer in 1974 leaving him and his brother Richard, both teenagers. Outside of the official palace and other residences that his father left behind, Ronnie wanted this house which was his mother's home to be his official private home because he had that special attachment.

Several days before the wedding, my friend Joyce Kisubi who was working closely with Mr Mulwana, the chairman of the wedding committee, had suggested that I should go and see how my home-to-be had been transformed. It had been rebuilt, refurbished and furnished in preparation for our arrival. She was right. I was pleased with what I saw—quite different from the first time.

Now here I was, the night of our wedding right after the reception seated in the living room of Kireka Palace with the wedding party entourage. Harriet Masembe took photographs, which turned out to be the most precious of gifts since no official photographs had been taken after we had lost out our official photographer in the maze. We actually took our portraits weeks after the wedding. Yes, the Kabaka and I had to wear our wedding outfits again!

The people of Buganda insisted on financing their Kabaka's wedding. The Katikiro had set up a preparation committee with Mr James Mulwana as the chair and treasurer.

'People contributed willingly. I actually don't know anyone who didn't. The problem was that everybody insisted on handing the money to me, which was a lot of work. People brought cows, goats, and all sorts of things. Organisations such as MTN, breweries, and

many other big corporations donated and happily volunteered to carry out certain tasks during the wedding. The wedding went on very well. We had guests
who came from Nigeria, Sudan, Ethiopia, Rwanda,
Burundi, including all the kingdoms in Uganda; but
had the wedding taken place two days later than it did,
I would have broken down. It was unbelievable'!

–J.G. Mulwanyammuli Ssemwogerere
(Katikiro/Prime Minister Buganda Kingdom 1994-2005)

Someone reading is probably thinking, *I bet you couldn't wait to
leave everything and fly way to some quiet place for your honeymoon.* Well,
I wish we had. It was not until four months later in January
that we were able to steal away and have a proper honeymoon
in Nairobi and Mombasa, Kenya.

But wait…let me tell you about one more ceremony that
we had a month after the wedding. We call it *okuzza omuzigo.*
It is the customary closure to the marriage festivities, where I,
the bride, get to prepare a meal for my new husband's family.
I remember the mammoth cookout with my aunties.

On September 1, 1999, the *Monitor* newspaper published the
following: "The wedding of Buganda's Kabaka Ronnie Mutebi
to Sylvia Nagginda Luswata last Friday, an event which some
estimate attracted over 1 million people to Namirembe hill
and the Lubiri, was possibly the second most covered Ugandan
story in the last 30 years."

'On Saturday, I ran an Internet search and virtually
every major English newspaper in the world, from the
prestigious *Washington Post* (that later ran a full-page

story of the wedding and likened it to a fairy tale), to the prestigious *Guardian* in the UK, a bunch of papers in Australia and Canada, and several television networks including CNN (where the story ran for two days), and radio stations carried a story of the Mutebi-Luswata wedding'.

—John Mukalazi Kamya (Former Employer, Friend)

'I was shocked when I heard about her marrying the Kabaka. I feared it would change her. It was refreshing to see her shortly after the wedding in Sweden. I expected her to be very different, maybe untouchable. And why not? She was after all, a queen now. She was the Nnaabagereka of Buganda. To my pleasant surprise, she hadn't changed at all. She was still the Sylvia I had grown to love and care for. She was and still is a woman of great character, who is always friendly, warm, calm, loving and extremely generous'.

—Robinah Mukasa (Friend)

'I travelled to Uganda for the wedding, and I was not at all surprised. Here was a couple who were suited for each other. They both grew up with a strong sense of Kiganda decorum, and both had lived abroad since their teenage years. Sylvia Nagginda had been raised to be a Buganda king's wife, and the education, poise, and success she acquired in the USA made her particularly suitable to marry a king. In a way, the girl born and raised to be a queen, indeed became one'.

—Jean Sembeguya Matovu (Friend)

# ELIZABETH OF TOORO

'It was clear that Kabaka's wedding inspired an unprecedented spirit of reconciliation and mutual respect amongst Ugandans in a way that had not been witnessed in the recent history of the country. There seemed to be near national consensus that this was a day of Buganda's pride, which in a peculiar way radiated to the whole country without arousing the slightest controversy. The wedding also strengthened ties between the other Kingdom areas of Uganda.'
   –Katikiro Charles Peter Mayiga, in "King on the Throne"

Historically, the Buganda Kingdom has enjoyed a flourishing friendship with the Tooro Kingdom. Princess Elizabeth Bagaya of Tooro has been a consistent friend to the Kabaka, me and members of the Buganda royal family through good and bad times. Elizabeth Bagaya was the *Batebe* (Princess Royal under Omukama Kaboyo) of the Kingdom of Toro. She is a paternal aunt to the current King of Tooro, Oyo Nyimba Kabamba Iguru Rukidi.

Her love for Buganda dates back to the 1950s, when she spent a good part of her childhood in the Buganda royal palace at Mengo. Princess Elizabeth Bagaya has fond memories of Kabaka Mutesa and the royal family, many of whom became her lifelong friends including Princesses Sarah Kagere, Dorothy Nasolo, Agnes Nabaloga, and Dina Kigga, my sisters-in-law. She speaks passionately about Baganda, praising our culture and recognising our intelligence, governance and hospitality.

The princess speaks fondly of her mother's—Abwooli Kezia Byanjeru—friendship with the Kabaka Mutesa's wife, Nnaabagereka Damali Kisosonkole. She once said, 'They laughed and cried together as women married to kings of "many considerations"'.

For long, I had admired Princess Bagaya from afar—her stunning beauty and wit. I often thought, *How can someone be so beautiful and intelligent!*

When we finally met much later in my life, it was as though we had known each other all our lives. After all, I was married into a family that she so much loved; and it so happened she already had connections within my side of the family. She had walked in my uncle Dan Sebugwawo's wedding as the maid of honour. She had gone on to make so many friends with my senior aunts. Over the years, we would become very close and forged a much-treasured friendship.

> 'Nnaabagereka's aunts were known to me and my siblings. She's a very good friend of Tooro Kingdom where she has attended a number of Omukama's coronation anniversary functions. I had special relationships with Namasole Irene, Kabaka Mutesa II's mother and Nnaabagereka Damali Mutesa's wife. To be a Kabaka's wife is a respectable yet very difficult position. I believe Nnaabagereka Nagginda's era has just started and still has a huge responsibility. I pray that God stays with her and shows her the way'.
> —Princess Elizabeth Bagaya (Friend)

Elizabeth of Tooro, as she became known around the world, is a Ugandan lawyer, politician, diplomat, model and actress.

Even with all the pomp, glamour, distinctions, and royalty, she is the most cultured and most humble person I have ever met. She stands tall, depicting what a cultured upbringing of *obuntubulamu* combined with a good education can yield. She is a traditionalist in love with her Kitoro culture and yearns for a more developed, progressive and stronger Toro Kingdom.

> 'I would like to see our cultural institutions especially the traditional Kingdoms of Buganda, Tooro, Ankole and Bunyoro, along with the Chiefdom of Busoga work together for the good of all Ugandans'.
> —Princess Elizabeth Bagaya (Friend)

## IN HINDSIGHT

Our wedding was nothing that I ever dreamt of or hoped for. They say that literally hundreds of thousands of people attended the live festivities, with millions more watching via television. I could only clearly understand the magnitude after watching the video recordings.

On that day, my life as an ordinary girl ceased, and I stepped into a large, undefined role. I assumed responsibilities for the people of Buganda, along with the high expectations that accompany my position. Without grasping it then, that was the beginning of the realisation of my dream. The dream to play a critical role in the development of my country which I had spelt out over thirteen years prior to the wedding in my undergraduate paper on 'Communication for Development'.

After eighteen years in the United States, a new chapter was beginning: an exciting chapter that challenges conventional wisdom on how change can happen in the 21$^{st}$ century. As a queen in a traditional cultural institution, I was placed close to the apex of a traditional cultural value system in a modern world and, above all, put in a position that would build both my personal leadership aptitude, and my African woman's collective leadership prowess.

Prior to my marriage, I didn't take time to think hard about what I was getting into. At 36 years of age, I just wanted to get married. I therefore walked in without any formed thoughts about this gigantic role. I honestly thought I was just coming to get married, have kids, and offer some services to my husband's enormous work which would in turn contribute to the development of our country.

Since there hadn't been a Nnaabagereka in Buganda or Uganda for thirty-three years, I had no good sense of what it really meant to the people of Buganda. Neither did I receive any special preparations or briefings that one would expect to be given to a king's bride-to-be.

After the abolition of kingdoms in Uganda in 1966, the Buganda royal household system broke down completely. The complex system which had been the pride of many nations and admired by many people around the world was no more. The Kingdom was restored in 1993 and at the time of our wedding in 1999, it was still rising from its ashes. Therefore, orienting the Nnaabagereka to her position was certainly not a priority, and it is also possible that no one really knew what it entailed.

I didn't have much time to settle into my new role, not only as a wife, but as the wife of a king. There was the myriad of duties in service to a people who had shown me such tremendous love and support, the demand for my time in the different parts of the Kingdom, and the hundreds of invitations from various institutions and organisations to officiate at their events and functions.

So, I jumped in with sleeves rolled up to serve the best way that I could, without giving much thought to all the obstacles I might encounter. I chose not to consider the male prejudices that might exist after 800-plus years of ingrained patriarchal institutionalism. I was somewhat oblivious to the dangers ahead. It never occurred to me that my good intentions would likely be misunderstood by some people.

As the Nnaabagereka of Buganda, I enjoyed many opportunities, but also faced countless challenges. The title Nnaabagereka is derived from the Luganda word *Okugereka*, which literally means 'to prepare' and 'to apportion', but loosely means 'to serve people'. Henceforth, my dreams and aspirations of wanting to work with and to serve the people were met—this was a major bridge in my life.

Looking back, I was unknowingly being guided by the hand of God. Had I approached my role from a purely logical, analytical perspective, I would have likely failed miserably. Like a child who is learning to walk and clings onto the grownups completely oblivious to the dangers and challenges ahead, my innocence became my strength as I grew into my role.

'I believe that her days in New York City and work at the United Nations prepared her for her current role as Nnaabagereka, a huge responsibility which she has taken on with grace and humility. Her spirituality keeps her grounded. Her love and commitment to other people is real, pure and simply amazing! She is always looking out for others to ensure that all is well'.

–Lydia Kibedi (Friend)

# chapter 11

# EZZADDE
(Children)

After our wedding, I tried to do life as a normal citizen, but soon realised that I couldn't. I remember trying to go incognito to the supermarket a few times. Didn't work. As soon as someone realised who I was, they'd call their friends and before long, they would crowd the aisles with paparazzi in the wings. I didn't feel like I was in danger, but it felt awkward.

'Having been in His Majesty's royal service for a very long time, I started to get to know the Nnaabagereka up close personally and most especially when she accompanied the Kabaka to Sweden on her first international royal tour, shortly after the wedding. One thing was clear: Many of us had asked God for a Nnaabagereka. Without a doubt, our Heavenly Father had responded by giving us a most precious gift in Sylvia Nagginda, our beloved Maama. Almost immediately, she had captured the hearts of many with her self-discipline, unquestioning loyalty, and devotion to King and Country'.

—The Venerable Archdeacon
Emeritus Prince Daniel Kajumba

'I was both surprised and excited to hear that she was getting married to the Kabaka. A year after the wedding, I was thrilled to receive her invitation to attend the Kabaka's birthday dinner at their residence in Kireka. We've kept in touch since. She has been a very good friend to me; really down to earth despite who she is'.

—Justine Nakato Katto (Friend)

## BANAKAZADE (Mothers)

*Banakazade*, meaning "Mothers", was an organisation of distinguished ladies of high profile within the Buganda society. The group felt that as a young mother, still a newlywed, with daunting responsibilities ahead of me and in an environment that was just getting used to having a Nnaabagereka again after thirty-three years, desperately needed all the support and encouragement I could get. Given their experience as mothers, wives and workers, they became my mentors and advisors, tirelessly offering the critical support system I so desperately needed.

Among the Banakazade was Rebecca Mulira who had served as a women's rights advocate and social activist involved in the Ugandan Women's movement from the 1950s to the '80s.

She was also Kabaka's aunt. She loved us to bits and was extremely devoted to the Kabakaship. She was relentless in her efforts to make sure that the welfare in the palace was safe-guarded. Together with Mrs Edith Kassede, they grew a garden that provided bananas and vegetables to the palace whenever needed. Other Banakazade members included: Syda Bbumba, Lydia Balemezi, Solome Bossa, Josephine Kabanda, Evelyn Kaggwa, Sarah Mulwana, Joyce Mpanga, Solome Mpanga, Lydia Mugambi, Betty Mugoya, Mary Mulumba, Maria Mutagamba, Racheal Sematimba, Julia Sebutinde, Rita Matovu, Margaret Zziwa, Miriam Kavuma, Gladys Wambuzi, Rhoda Nsibambi, and Ruth Nkoyoyo. I will always be grateful for the love and support they showed me.

Tragically, Rebecca's life was cut short on my birthday, November 9, 2001, in a car accident. Just the day before, she had passed by the palace to drop off a birthday cake for me. I wasn't home. When I called to thank her the following morning, she was travelling by car to a relative's funeral in Masaka. She said, 'I had to bring your cake early since I am travelling today'. Naturally, I wished her safe travels. Later that evening, I received a call from her son, Ham, that they had been involved in an accident and his mum had passed away. I was totally devastated.

The dreadful call came in as I was heading out to a birthday dinner that was organised by Nakimera Kanyerezi, Masembe Kanyerezi and his wife, and other friends including Michael Kyompi Sebalu, Tom Kiggundu with his wife Julie. Since several attendees knew Rebecca, I chose to not cancel, but attend to be close to those who knew Rebecca.

## FAMILY

The Kabaka and I have a blended family. This means that from day one, I was a mother to three amazing children, Junju, Joan and Victoria. They have been a blessing in my life.

Suffice to say, I thought Ronnie had one child, our son, Junju. He never mentioned the other kids until our last London visit a few months before the wedding. So I asked, 'Ronnie, how many children do you really have'?

'Three', he said.

'Three'? I quizzed.

'Yes', he replied, 'but most people don't know the other two—they're girls'.

I was quiet for a few minutes, hoping he would say he was just kidding. He didn't. He wasn't kidding. That rattled me for a bit, although I never mentioned it to him. I thought to myself, *How am I going to raise three stepchildren, moreover from three different women?* I ruminated on this over several months. At some point, and I am not sure at exactly when, the issue became inconsequential to my decision to proceed with our relationship.

My first order of business was to try as best as I could to connect with them. My strict upbringing and work ethic had made a rather strict disciplinarian out of me. So, with me came rules that the kids didn't quite welcome.

Kabaka's first-born child is Junju.

'I had heard the rumours of a budding love relationship between my dad and mom. Eventually, he sat me down and made it official. Naturally, I was excited for him and for our family too. I was only 14 years old. Mom and I set off on the right foot, as she sought friendship and connection. Eventually, we became the best of friends. My problem was the discipline. Dad is really laid back. He will advise you, but generally prefers to allow you to self-correct. Not her. She was pretty strict! She introduced curfews. Much as I understood her position, I felt like I was grown enough to do whatever I wanted to do. I wasn't a kid anymore. But eventually, I began to submit to order. I understood that I needed the discipline and boundaries, not just for the proper functioning of our household, but as a life skill. I learnt that this had to be a two-way street. Much as I wanted her to understand me, I had to also understand her. I learnt to negotiate, and not make demands. I knew that she loved me and wasn't trying to squash my desires. The discipline was for my protection, not control. Most importantly, I determined that however wide the rift or deep the conflict between us, respect for her was simply not an option. The same goes for my dad. I need their voice in my life. Bottom line is being "my own man", as we guys like to put it these days, doesn't mean disrespect for my parents. Just because I am all grown up doesn't mean that I can talk to my dad or mom like they are my peers. Mom is amazing. Looking back at her journey and what she has accomplished, I have great respect and admiration for her. She is our mother. But not only that, she is the mother of an entire Kingdom of millions of people. I am supremely proud of her achievements'.

—Prince Junju Kiweewa (Stepson)

Next, there is Joan.

'I was 9 years old when she came into our lives. She was stunning both outside and inside. I remember shopping for dresses and the fun of it all. It was amazing! I still remember her wedding dress; a fusion of our local busuuti and conventional gowns. I still remember the long train. I had never seen anything like that. Almost immediately, she would become a role model to me on so many levels. I call her my support system. She has been a personal mentor, showing me the ropes on my developmental journey. Unlike a stereotypical authoritarian African mother, she always seeks to understand first. We have talked through many issues and with her gentle demeanor, she has helped me synthesise solutions that work for both of us. She is careful not to impose her perspective upon us. That's pretty impressive to me. It has taught me to ask harder questions of myself. She was funny too. I remember her telling us that Shaggy, the reggae superstar, was a distant cousin. "Hey, I will call him if you like", she said. She picked up her cell phone and dialed. She then had this long casual back and forth conversation, until my brother decided to call her phone. Needless to say, she was busted! When people ask me what it's like to be a princess, I really don't know what to say because I don't know what it's like to be anything else.

Thankfully, I have had opportunities to get out of this bubble. I have been to school in Kenya, England and the USA. In fact, like her, I went to NYU. And guess what—I also interned at the United Nations. It has been so good to see her impact on our culture. She represents a fresh, cool way of doing royalty. She is truly a modern African queen. I am so proud of her'!

–Princess Joan Nassolo (Stepdaughter)

Last, but certainly not least, there is Vicky.

'I was 9 years old when she came into our lives. My birth mother passed away five years later. I struggled with her boundaries and her rules. I was a teenager trying to grapple with deep loss; but hard as I was, she never gave up on me. The press has referred to me as the "black sheep of the family". Maybe because I get suffocated by the protocols and people's expectations of me. I generally prefer to do things my way—always have! I could see that she also wasn't playing by the rules. She didn't just want to be dad's wife or stay in her box as the Nnaabagereka. She wanted to make a real difference for Buganda and the country. So, she didn't fight me. She listened to me and tried to get into my space. She showed me persistent love and really tried to understand me, which eventually won me over. This is something I wish other mothers could do. Young people want to be listened to, most of all. Try and listen to your kids before you judge or punish them. Today I call her mom, but also friend. I know for a fact that she is there for me, regardless. She is an amazing woman. She has been a great addition to our family. Even more, she has been a tremendous blessing to the country'.

—Princess Victoria Nkinzi (Stepdaughter)

## KATRINA-SARAH

I remember when I found out that I was pregnant. This was another dream come true. Since I was a child, I dreamt of having my own kids. So yes, I was so thrilled, but also terrified. *What if I lose the baby? What if there are complications? What if I can't do this?* My mind was filled with all kinds of thoughts.

So, I didn't tell Ronnie until after the first trimester. I didn't want to start a frenzy, but most importantly, I really wanted to relish this time as a personal journey. I decided to work from our residence away from peering eyes, lest some inquisitive reporter noticed my bulging belly. I am so grateful to Dr Batwaala who took the best care of me.

Once I broke the news to Ronnie, he immediately shared the news with his family. I flew to Nairobi, Kenya, for a full prenatal exam. I learnt that God had given us a daughter, something I kept to myself until the end. I didn't want to create a fuss about it. I didn't even tell Ronnie.

I made one public appearance at six months, and the following day all news outlets carried the announcement. 'A royal baby is to come', they broadcasted. The media frenzy I had tried to avoid erupted.

Shortly after that, I decided to go to London, England, to prepare for our daughter's arrival. Accompanying me was Jessica Bisaso, the *Nnabikande*, the 'royal midwife', a relative from the Kabaka's mother's side, traditionally responsible for the safe delivery of the royal child. I also travelled with my cousin, my personal assistant Cate Bwete, and to act as nanny was Betty Nakijoba. Mr. Ahmed Bamweyana facilitated our arrival at the airport. He was very helpful throughout our stay.

'In 2001, Ssabasajja Kabaka asked me to look after HRH in London as she prepared to deliver her new baby. I was immediately very anxious about this enormous responsibility. We created 'Operation Ttu (Parcel)', which included Edgar Kavuma, Maureen Kiyingi, Cate Bwete, Jessica Bisaso (Nabikande), Betty Nakijoba, Ruth Kajumba, Owek. late John Magoye and Nsambu Musisi, the Nteges, the Mukiibis, among others. It wasn't until we met her and realised just how humble and human she was that I began to relax. I noted that she purposely went to great lengths to put people at ease'.

–The Venerable Archdeacon
Emeritus Prince Daniel Kajumba

I enjoyed the quietude and solitude of Bayswater, an area in the city of Westminster in West London. I remember taking brisk walks in Hyde Park. I loved to shop for our baby girl. It is then that my assistants started to get suspicious because even though I was buying too many neutral or white outfits, I was more curious about those pink dresses. I cherish those memories to this very day.

'Finding a suitable residence for HRH and her entourage was tricky given the need for privacy for this one of the most iconic figures in Uganda and Africa. We also had to decide on an appropriate hospital cognisant of the need to avoid local press in UK and at home in Uganda'.
—The Venerable Archdeacon
Emeritus Prince Daniel Kajumba

As the day approached, Mum, Reuben and Ssenga Catherine Bamundaga flew in from the USA to stay with me.

'I was determined not to miss the next big thing. So, I flew to London with my mother to welcome her into motherhood. What a moment! My sister was a mother...yeah'!
—Reuben Codjoe (Brother)

They helped me walk through the final days of the journey. I remember going through name books. Initially, I chose the name Esther, but I was outvoted. They thought it was an old name. We settled on Katrina which also meant Catherine, my grandmother's name. We decided to hyphenate her name to add Sarah after her paternal grandmother and my great grandmother Sarah, Maama's mother, a favoured name by both our families.

'She was careful to choose neutral colours, so I couldn't guess the sex of the baby. We didn't know she already knew. I don't know how she managed to keep such a big secret. I remember the day she was admitted to Queen Charlotte's & Chelsea Hospital in Hammersmith. We prayed before she was wheeled away into the delivery room, along with the Nnabikande, the royal midwife'.

—Cate Nabankema Bwete (Cousin)

On July 4, 2001, at 10:40 a.m., Katrina-Sarah was born at Queen Charlotte's & Chelsea Hospital in Hammersmith, London.

'Finally, our joy was complete. I was privileged to lead the prayers when Ssanga was born and therefore hold the attendance record of all present. We prayed a blessing for the baby and her parents. We prayed that Ssanga finds delight, receives support, carries hope and knows God's love. We gave thanks and praise to God for the gift of this baby and for creating her in His image, and for the gift of life and love that had brought this beautiful baby girl here to us on earth. It was so surreal when years later, I was involved identifying for her a suitable university. Who would look after her? They had to learn to love Manchester United, her favourite team soccer team'.

—The Venerable Archdeacon
Emeritus Prince Daniel Kajumba

Traditionally, the Kabaka names his children in a special ceremony. But being in London, we had to give Katrina-Sarah a last name for her birth certificate. Consequently, her original birth certificate reads Katrina-Sarah Mirembe Kirabo.

'We stayed in London for another three months to enable the Nnaabagereka to fully recover. Meanwhile, the press was going crazy. There were stories of babies being switched around, of her giving birth to an albino, and so on. It was comical'.

—Cate Nabankema Bwete (Cousin)

After the baby was vaccinated and strong enough to fly home, we were ready to travel back to Uganda in September—9/11 happened just a few days before our planned departure.

The September 11, 2001, attacks were a series of four coordinated suicide terrorist attacks carried out by the militant Islamic extremist network al-Qaeda against the United States. I was shocked, heartbroken as I witnessed the tragic events unfold in real time on television, around my former home, New York. I was sitting in the living room with Namasole Rebecca Musoke who had come to see the baby. Namasole was the heir to Kabaka's mother and hence took on the role of Namasole which means mother to the Kabaka or King.

After we returned home, I had to continue with the recommended vaccination and general medical care regiment. I needed a doctor. My friend Barbara recommended her family paediatrician, Dr Kasirye. Dr Kasirye was an excellent doctor whom I have also recommended to many other mothers.

Later in September, our daughter was officially named by her father—*Ssangalyambogo*. When I asked Ronnie what it meant, he said *maanyi*, meaning 'strength'. Incidentally, sometime the previous year, as Cate and I were looking through a list of names for Baganda royalty, we came across a number of names which we thought were 'strange'—and *Ssangalyambogo* was one of them. We even laughed about it. Little did I know that my daughter would carry the same name. True to her name, *Ssanga*, as we normally call her, is a strong and independent young lady. In fact, most of the time she knows exactly what she wants and is not easily swayed.

'Mom shines when she enters a room. Confident, imposing but graceful, nonetheless. Oh, and she can be fun too. A few years ago, I managed to trick her into riding a rollercoaster with me in Dubai. I will never forget the look on her face when we got down to the end of the ride. "Never again", she vowed. She is determined to make a lady out of me. I can always hear her in my head: "Sit up straight"! "Be careful who you hang out with". "Don't say that"! "Don't do that"! I couldn't become the woman I am destined to be without her firm but gentle hand. Typically, if you are not a doctor, lawyer, accountant, or architect here in Africa, you are pretty much stuck. Thankfully, I have a mom who has been incredibly supportive. As a result, I have found my lane in the creative arts. I am also a swimmer. Both she and Dad have supported me and, in fact, pushed me to excel. Consequently, I have risen to win in the nationals to represent Uganda on a global stage. In a way, I so wish this for other families. I would like for us as a nation to begin to value the creative arts and encourage our kids to pursue their passions, even when they are outside of the mainstream'.

–Princess Katrina-Sarah Ssangalyambogo (Daughter)

On December 6, 2010, I was blessed with two more girls Jade Nakato and Jasmine Babirye born in Kampala Women's International Hospital—twins with completely different personalities. They're two amazing kids who are mostly happy and are passionate about people which, at their age, I find astounding.

Let me tell you a little bit about them.

Jade Nakato is indifferent, cuddly and extremely loving. With open-wide hands, she greets and hugs just about everybody she meets including complete strangers, which we thought was dangerous. While walking in the garden one day, Jade saw the garden man, Kalibala, working. His clothes and hands soiled. With open hands, she quickly went up to hug him in her loving way. I was repulsed by her gesture. Her nanny Josey shouted, 'Jade, you're going to catch diseases'! I quickly added, 'Jade, it's not good to go around hugging everybody. You really need to stop doing that', I reprimanded her. She ran away upset. I later found her in a corner crying. When I asked, she sobbed, 'I don't know why I do it, I just find myself doing it...it is God who tells me. God says you should love people'. I couldn't believe what I was hearing from this little four-year-old child. I stepped back and asked God to forgive me. *God, protect these little children,* I thought.

Jasmine Babirye, on the other hand, is extremely cautious yet equally loving and confident. She has so many questions to ask and countless stories to tell. I remember when she exclaimed to my shock that she didn't want to go to Heaven: 'Because one has to die to get there, and I don't want to die'! she explained.

Richard Semakokiro is my other stepchild. He is growing up alongside his cousin brother Grace Nsubuga. The two are smart and inseparable, with lots of energy as boys will always be boys. They love cartoons, gadgets and cars.

# chapter 12

# EMIRIMU
## (Work)

'I remember when she asked me to find her a personal assistant. Turns out that person was me. Initially, it was just me and her sitting on the same table in Kireka, until we moved to Bulange. Straight from the get-go, she jumped right in. She does not want to be a fixture. She loves people, which compels her to doggedly serve them. Interestingly, some have complained that her hard work diminished her dignity. That couldn't be further from the truth. HRH is a woman of excellence. When she wants something done, it's got to be done right, even if it means doing it several times over. She is committed to process and integrity. Her ethics will not allow her to bend rules or blur lines. That makes her special. Although very meticulous, she is fairly easy to work with. She will tell you exactly what she wants and when you miss it'.

—Cate Nabankema Bwete (Personal Assistant)

# OFFICE

The Office of the Nnaabagereka is a new phenomenon in Buganda Kingdom. The previous Nnaabagereka, Damali, was involved in promoting social welfare through various community interventions. However, she didn't hold or have an operational office per se.

Within the establishment, some key people believed that the Nnaabagereka wasn't supposed to hold a formal office. Therefore, to some extent, my efforts were initially perceived as taboo. As a result, there was constant internal effort to discourage its existence, and to bring it down, even after it was established.

Suffice to say, I was initially unaware of this sabotage. I honestly thought that the establishment was supportive of my efforts since my aim and devotion as Nnaabagereka was to complement the work of Ssabasajja Kabaka by serving our people of Buganda and the nation as a whole.

Having lived in the United States most of my adult life, I was generally oblivious to potential taboos. Besides, no one pointed them out to me. Keep in mind, we hadn't had a Kabaka in more than thirty years. In many ways, we were in uncharted territory.

Although not directly, in the early years of its establishment, the Office of the Nnaabagereka wasn't recognised or accepted in the official set up of the Kingdom's administration. Many times, it was hard to get resources to facilitate our work within my office. Worse still, some of our adversaries told the Kabaka that the Nnaabagereka was acting in bad faith; that I was trying to set up a parallel institution, something that consequently reflected negatively on our marriage. The subtle, yet clear message was that I wasn't welcome within the main establishment.

To my knowledge, the Kabaka himself didn't have a problem with the existence of my office, which tremendously helped in anchoring my courage to move on with its establishment. I was also encouraged by public and close support groups—in addition to my own determination not to pay attention to diversions. My innocence and oblivion to the ill intentions and the cynicism aimed at me or my work bolstered my confidence and sharpened my focus. I believed in our mission. Moreover, I knew that it would benefit the Kingdom.

One of the main instructions that I gave to my office was that we needed to keep communication lines open between us and the office of the Kabaka and the Katikiro (Prime Minister). We updated them of our work and informed them of any official events that I attended. With much perseverance, we successfully worked hard to keep the Office of the Nnaabagereka alive over the years.

My first private secretary was Helen Bossa, a soft-spoken lady who helped me organize office systems and manage my first projects. She was instrumental in setting up the office. About five years later, God sent Juliet Ssenteza my way. She has been a faithful confidant even at the time of this writing.

'I had observed her at a distance. I was attracted to her authenticity. She was our Queen—The Nnaabagereka—the most powerful woman in our tribe, our Maama, completely culturally far removed from any of us commoners. *Will I ever get close to her?* I wondered. I remember a particular function at my daughter's school where she was the guest speaker. Right in the middle of it all, the rain began to pour down hard. Everyone took cover, but I would not budge. I took my chair and held it over my head as a makeshift umbrella. She wasn't frazzled either. She didn't seem to be irritated at all. She kept her composure to the surprise of everyone, except me. This right here is exactly who I thought she was. The woman I had been admiring: composed, dignified, touchable, yet sophisticated. *I have to work for her*, I determined. So, you can imagine my surprise when I was invited to interview at her office for a private secretary position. Yes, I was nervous, intimidated and completely out of my comfort zone, but I didn't waver. This was my destiny—to work for the Nnaabagereka. I did get the job and it has been everything I thought and more. She is the most generous person I know. She has sponsored countless ventures, funded numerous initiatives, paid for school fees for so many, all outside of the spotlight. She insists on keeping her benevolence private. She is driven by excellence; never overpromises yet always aiming to over deliver. She is not easy to please but is gracious when we miss it. She will solicit my opinion and that of others even when she knows what she must do. She will stand up for the defenceless and will not entertain slander, as she is a champion of truth both publicly and privately. She is a woman of God'.

—Juliet Ssenteza (Principal Private Secretary)

# THE KABAKA

As the Nnaabagereka, it was my pleasure and indeed duty to play a supportive role to the Kabaka, Ronald Muwenda Mutebi II, and the Buganda government. I was fascinated by the enduring strength of our great people. I was impressed by the passionate love that everyone had for our Kabaka. This monarchy was much different from the democracies I had been exposed to. While politicians have to persuade, arm-twist, even manipulate people to rally them around their causes, the Kabaka didn't. He simply needs to express his wishes, and in the simplest of ways, that wish was indeed perceived as a command. I was amazed, and still am, by the power and enormous influence of the king.

From time immemorial, the Baganda have traditionally identified with the Kabakaship as a source of core identity and as a rallying point and personification of their political, social, economic and cultural aspirations. To the Baganda, the Kabaka is an enduring source of inspiration and influence. He is held in high esteem and commands great respect and authority among his people, and indeed, all Ugandans. This conviction continues to be held by younger generations.

The Kabaka uses his authority to mobilise people for development—to promote unity, understanding and industriousness among his people.

'It was not until 2007 that I finally went to visit her in Uganda. Then it hit me! The entourage, police convoys, bodyguards—I was treated like royalty. Wait a minute, I was royalty. I had no idea how huge everything was. Being the queen's brother was a big deal, I guess. I was shocked to see the deep love and respect the people had for my sister. She was indeed the mother of the Kingdom. I remember meeting His Majesty the King. I didn't know whether to bow or say, "What's up, brother-in-law". He told me to relax. We hugged and what an experience! For three weeks, I met the scores of relatives, ate good food and had an unforgettable time! My big surprise was that Sylvia was still Sylvia. Even with the tremendous power that she had; she was still my big sis. But she had become more—a pivotal personality of our day; a powerful, charismatic, articulate, yet selfless leader'.

–Reuben Codjoe (Brother)

The structure of the Kingdom of Buganda is inclusive. Through the different clan heads, everyone is represented. They all carry a sense of belonging to the establishment. There are no classes among the Baganda, which means that the Kabaka can come from any clan.

Below the Kabaka, we have the head of the royals, then the chief clan head, the clan heads, the Prime Minister, the ministers, the county chiefs, and sub county chiefs. The top/down system allows the Buganda Kingdom to leverage its power and ability to mobilise and organise, in order to gain legitimacy as entrusted to it by the people. It is this structure that has been vital in enabling the mobilisation and association of people both within the region and throughout the country.

To this end, my office and the Nnabagereka Development Foundation have been effective partners for local and national leadership to effect positive change where it's needed. For example, where development programmes have been resisted, misunderstood, or not valued, I have come alongside the Kabaka to enhance communication and co-operation among the people. We have supported health programmes including immunisation, improved our environment by promoting forestation, advanced education for girls, and empowered women and youth with agricultural and business skills.

The Buganda Kingdom as a traditional cultural institution, embodies the identity and aspirations of its people; and consequently, even without legislative or administrative power, it commands the loyalty of millions.

'Although she describes herself as an "ordinary girl", she grew up as a member of the Buganda nobility. This has had a profound impact on her life. She is highly intelligent, motivated, articulate, and humble. I have watched her in amazement and admiration as she selflessly performs her duties while carving out a very distinct and modern role for the Nnaabagereka in Buganda, something that all those who truly love the Buganda in particular and Uganda in general, greatly appreciate'.

–The Venerable Archdeacon
Emeritus Prince Daniel Kajumba

## CALL TO ACTION

As I prayed about how to best serve, I started to think about my title, *The Nnaabagereka*. As mentioned previously, it is derived from the Luganda word, *Okugereka*, which literally means 'to serve'.

Nnaabagereka Nagginda the consort of Kabaka Ronald Mutebi II, is occupying a significant position in the Kingdom of Buganda.

When the Kingdom witnessed the Royal wedding on 27 August 1999, it created new dynamics and expectations from the King's Court. The Kingdom had just been restored six years before, after a 27-year interregnum, and this was arguably the right time for the people of Buganda to expect the institution to address serious social challenges that seemed to be compounded by the passage of time, and which could not be addressed through legislation.

Issues related to the family as the basic unit that upholds our heritage, and where grooming of children into focused and responsible subjects (and citizens), had been neglected for decades.

The Nnaabagereka rose to the challenge. She initiated programs that re-invigorate our centuries-old values of integrity, civility, empathy, respect, humility and hard work, among others, in children. She embarked on the girl-child and women projects intended to empower them, within our cultural frameworks, in order for them to be exposed to, and to exploit, the abundant opportunities, respectively. All these efforts are crucial if the Kingdom (and the country, Uganda) is to experience social and economic transformation. For all this, and more, I commend Nnaabagereka Nagginda. She has effectively complimented Kabaka Mutebi's efforts to bring our heritage close to the hearts of the people of Buganda. The decision to chronicle her experience in this role will significantly contribute to the annals of our history.

–Katikiro Charles Peter Mayiga
(Prime Minister, Buganda Kingdom)

I began to see my influence, and the enormous opportunities it afforded me. As the Nnaabagereka, everyone called me *Maama wa Buganda*, which as you may recall, means 'Mother of Buganda'. Initially, I resented the designation. I thought it aged me, especially when much older people used it. I even tried to stop them from using it. But eventually, I accepted it. It was out of respect that they all called me Maama.

'Eventually, she invited me over to visit her. *Should I kneel for her? Do I address her as Maama?* Just then, she said, "Come on, Lydia, you don't have to kneel". I was still conflicted because she is the Nnaabagereka—our mother. I remember her sitting next to me at my daughter's wedding ceremony. It was so touching to receive a framed copy of one of the main pictures along with hundreds of others from her. I did not lose my Sylvia. We still have endless conversations, and I am sure that if she could lose her security detail, we would go dancing just like old times. I am thankful that she has not forgotten us. She has remained simple and authentic. Indeed, she has gone the extra mile for Buganda and our nation'.

–Lydia Nakatude Sserebe (Friend)

Remember that my vision was to return home and do something great for my country, which was reeling with massive underdevelopment. Back in college, I had written many papers on becoming a change agent in Uganda from the perspective of either an entrepreneur, a corporate head, or development specialist. Clearly, being Nnaabagereka presented me with far greater opportunities to fulfil my passion. In other words, I was better positioned to influence change than I had ever dreamt.

As *Maama wa Buganda,* I was moved by the critical issues of concern to women, children, and youth. I listened to first-hand accounts and witnessed people's concerns.

The high maternal and infant mortality rates told the dark story of the general wellbeing of women in our nation. Mothers pleaded for healthier families, better schools, and affordable healthcare services for both them and their kids. Most women didn't have access to reproductive healthcare services. This, considering that Uganda has the second highest fertility rate in the world, with women bearing on average seven children.

Young people below 20 years old make up 60 percent of the nation's population. In fact, the average age of the entire population is 16.7. Every one of them naturally wants to acquire skills in order to enhance their opportunities for gainful employment or entrepreneurship. They also expressed concerns about securing sustainable employment and feeling excluded from participation in society.

The dire predicament of people with disabilities, lack of clean drinking water, and the appalling hygiene conditions in communities, localities and on the streets was alarming. There was rampant scenes of poverty with kids scrambling for food portions, with the majority living in squalid conditions; children walking miles barefooted to schools with cracked walls and windowless classrooms with no or limited access to healthcare or clean drinking water. We were in trouble.

These sad realities gave me an opportunity to get involved and contribute to improving the living conditions of people through my own organisation. The goal: to make focused contributions in the areas of education and health targeting children, youth and women.

One afternoon, a few months after the wedding, the Kabaka invited me to a meeting of the Kabaka Foundation, an organisation he started in 1995. There he introduced me to the board members and trustees, who included his sister Princess Dorothy Nasolo. I quietly sat in and observed the proceedings.

Later, I was approached by the Buganda Minister of Education John Chrysestom Muyingo asking me to spearhead a fundraiser for the Kabaka Education Fund. This fund was first established in 1955 during the reign of Kabaka Edward Muteesa II and was the pre-eminent instrument for helping the needy but bright students in the Buganda Kingdom to attain higher education. Currently, the fund focuses on improving the quality of life of the people of Buganda in particular, and Uganda as a whole, through accessible, high-quality education that is relevant to the needs of the society.

Minister Muyingo proposed that I invite high profile individuals within the community, especially private school owners, and ask them to contribute to the fund. Being new on the scene, I didn't know anybody significant, but Mr Muyingo believed that no one would decline an invitation from me. So he, together with Mr Jockey Sempijja and other Buganda Education commissioners, identified the individuals with whom I would have a conversation. In about one week I met with more than fifty individuals. Sure enough, it was a successful campaign that raised a lot of funds for the Kabaka Education Fund.

In 2000, a delegation from the United Nations Fund for Population Activities asked me to serve as their goodwill ambassador. I heartily accepted. My work involved advocacy for maternal health, as well as adolescent and sexual reproductive health which included promoting family planning—a topic that was somewhat culturally sensitive.

We launched an aggressive re-education campaign targeting both women and men, emphasising that we're not trying to stop them from having children but rather encouraging them to have those they can afford to give a quality lifestyle. I asked them to ponder these questions:

- What good is it to have ten kids crowded in a house without amenities, adequate clothing, healthy nutrition, or basic education?

- If they could, would they want to space out their children a bit more, so better care can be provided for them?

- What if we all turn our attention to quality parenting, and not just quantity?

- How about we provide our expectant mothers with pre-natal care to aid in healthy fetal development?

- How good it would be if expectant mothers gave birth in hospitals or medical clinics with adequate supplies and medical care, instead of having home births?

We took this message to villages, churches and homes within our districts throughout the Kingdom and other regions like Busoga and Tooro. Local leaders welcomed us with open arms.

'Sylvia continues to use the leadership skills and values that her grandmother Kasalina instilled in her. We have witnessed her good work to improve the lives of boys, girls and teenagers in our communities benefiting not only Buganda but all other regions. She has become a beloved figure throughout Uganda'.

—Ann-Loi Nangendo Fulu (Aunt)

## PATRON

In 2000, Justice Solome Bossa, Sarah Bagalaaliwo and Sarah Mangale—three notable women of influence within our community—approached me about an idea. 'We think you should start an NGO'!

'Well, you couldn't have come at a better time', I replied. 'I have been thinking about doing exactly that, and as a matter of fact, I already have a draft concept', I told them.

They immediately volunteered to help me. I was thrilled to get such experienced ladies offering their assistance at a time when I hardly knew people in the community. Being new on the scene, I didn't know many people outside of my family. They helped me put the board together. Two of them were lawyers, so they advised on registration and other legalities. The organisation was registered, and meetings started taking place at least once a month during the first year. Sarah Bagalaaliwo kindly let us use her home in Kololo to hold the first meetings. There was high enthusiasm among the members.

We agreed the organisation would be called the Nnabagereka Development Trust (NDT), later becoming The Nnabagereka Development Trust Foundation (NDTF), and in 2007 changing to The Nnabagereka Development Foundation (NDF).

They also helped recommend key influencers, whom I personally invited to serve on our board of directors. I consulted the Kabaka as I selected prospective board members, and he was in agreement.

The organisation would serve as a vehicle through which I could help improve the quality of life of children, youth and women. We selected eleven board members and established a secretariat. We received seed capital from the Rockefeller Foundation and some well-wishers, plus of course, the Kabaka who gave me his office in Radiant House on Plot 20 Kampala Road to use as office space for the Foundation.

'We hadn't had a Nnaabagereka for thirty-three years, so she really had no one to train or mentor her. "I want to start something to help the marginalised in the Kingdom", she announced. She had just been married. *Hmmm....different!* I thought. I replied, "Well, but Ugandans don't have much of a reputation for philanthropy". "I know", she countered, "but you can help me try". I was challenged and inspired. Why should we always have to wait for handouts from the West? Isn't it time we moved our own business communities to action?

Can we not mobilise money from Africans for Africa?
All critical questions which moved me to action'.
                    —Honourable Maria Kiwanuka
            (Trustee Nnabagereka Development Foundation)

For the first time in my life, and without prior experience, I was heading an organisation. I researched and read a lot about the subject. I consulted experts, elders, as well as our founding members especially the three ladies. I thanked God for surrounding me with experienced people who guided me and helped me find my footing. I will forever be grateful to Justice Solome Bossa, Sarah Bagalaaliwo and Sarah Mangale. Others on the first board who were instrumental in helping me start the foundation were Arthur Bagunywa, Nnalyinya Sarah Kagere, Abdu Kagga, Judith Kamanyi, Maria Kiwanuka, Mary Mutyaba, and Aloysius Semmanda.

Notwithstanding, the board wasn't exactly sure how to relate to the Nnaabagereka as the principal in the organisation. They felt that my position would compromise my role. The solution, they suggested, was to appoint me as patron. Grateful as I was for their sensitivity, I felt like patron was too ceremonial and rather limited. You see, a patron doesn't engage in policy decisions, nor does she sit on the board. I wanted to actively and directly engage in the attainment of my vision—not that I didn't trust the board members. Some members objected to this.

Raising funds proved to be an enormous challenge and barely two years after we launched, most of the original board members lost interest and many stopped participating. Funds had been depleted, without any systems established or competent staff at the secretariat to run the organisation.

Suddenly, I was glad I hadn't disengaged as advised.

I took action with the handful of members who had remained. Since I had been attending meetings, I knew exactly how to move forward. My education background in communication and work experience came in handy. I believed in our cause which motivated me to keep my dream alive with barely any funds to run the foundation, much less pay our two staff-member secretariat. How did we do it? Persistence: never losing sight of the goal in spite of the challenges.

'I was initially concerned about her role. I knew she was not going to be an ordinary queen. I also wondered if she would be too disruptive to the status quo. Thankfully, she has been both tactful and sensitive. Being Nnaabagereka has given her a longer helping hand to the needy. Her impact has been extremely positive, both within Buganda and beyond. You see, women's issues are women's issues, whether one is a Muganda or not. Similarly, kids' issues are kids' issues, regardless of tribe or race'.

—Namata Katongole (Friend)

## THE NNABAGEREKA DEVELOPMENT FOUNDATION

The Nnabagereka Development Foundation is tasked with responding to the needs within our focus areas: children, women, and youth. We have been actively involved in numerous youth, health and educational initiatives throughout the country.

'In establishing the Foundation, Queen Sylvia was redefining the role of the Nnaabagereka. She moved it from its traditional limited space into the public sphere of a "working queen". She has made the title more relevant and enhanced its meaning and outlook. She's a leader and champion for promoting indigenous African culture and its role in development. In line with her beliefs and humility, she demonstrates a leadership style that is patient and humble and respects all in her team. On the international scene, she's a strong advocate of culture as a vehicle for addressing development needs and shares the need to revive and celebrate cultural values in the world'.

—Elizabeth Lwanga (Governance Board Member
Nnabagereka Development Foundation )

It has been more than twenty years now, and we're still going strong.

Our vision is to serve as a leading African foundation celebrating positive culture and providing sustainable development solutions. Our mission is to leverage culture to improve the economic and social wellbeing of children, youth, and women. To achieve these objectives, the Foundation purposefully ensures that the design and implementation of its development programme is informed by voices that are rooted in culture. We aim to catalyse a sense of dignity and pride in our people to engage as custodians of the rich cultural heritage of the Kingdom of Buganda, which has made tremendous contributions to the socio-economic development of Uganda as a whole.

'She had just finished a short-term marketing assignment with Uganda Manufacturers Association in 1993 when we first met. It was several years later in 2000 that our paths crossed again. She invited me to serve on the board of directors of the Nnabagereka Development Trust. Without hesitation, I agreed. Why? First of all, my grandfather had served as the permanent secretary of the Buganda treasury. My dad was friends to King Muteesa II. So, it seemed natural for me to serve the Crown just as well. Her invitation was an opportunity for me to give back to the less privileged. She believed that if we could impact our kids, women and the youth, it would go a long way to restoring our beloved Kingdom which was in shambles'.

–Judy Kamanyi (Trustee Nnabagereka
Development Foundation)

The Foundation facilitates national processes that use the 'cultural voice framework' for sustainable development which is clearly evident in the health and education sectors. I am a committed advocate for Sexual Reproductive Health (SRH), adolescent health, prevention of HIV/AIDS and other sexually transmitted diseases, promoting and supporting girl child education, skills enhancement and economic empowerment for youth and women.

'I am proud to see that we have provided quality primary education to vulnerable girls including children with disabilities. With funds from donors, we have guaranteed access to university education for girls with disadvantaged, socioeconomic backgrounds.

We have also been involved in successful national and grassroots level advocacy campaigns promoting sexual and reproductive health and rights. We have worked hard to expand income generation opportunities for women's groups'.

—Dr Jeff Sebuyira (Governance Board Chairperson Nnabagereka Development Foundation)

The Foundation promotes the establishment of nurturing and stimulating healthy environments for children, where learning is promoted, and physical and emotional needs met. We do this primarily to encourage and propel inter-generational transfer of affirmative behaviour and attitudes, knowledge, values and life skills.

'We got down to business, focusing our energies on the marginalised, both within the Kingdom of Buganda and without. For example, she highlighted the plight of refugee children in Northern Uganda. This was African philanthropy in action! We championed the cause of the girl-child and the boy-child. We advocated for women's rights. We even encouraged unemployed university and college graduates to stop loitering and look at vocational training— carpentry, welding, plumbing, and so on. Granted there was a lot of interest in these sidelined communities from other NGOs and global charities, but only the Nnaabagereka could bring her distinctively potent flavour of royalty and culture'.

—Honourable Maria Kiwanuka (Trustee Nnabagereka Development Foundation)

The Nnabagereka Development Foundation USA was incorporated in 2016 in New York as a nonprofit corporation limited by guarantee, and it is a chapter of the Nnabagereka Development Foundation in Uganda with autonomy in decision making, governance and accountability.

Purposes of the Foundation in the USA include:

1. Supporting the strategic objectives of the Foundation in Uganda taking into consideration the needs of the target beneficiaries and the economic, social and legal environment of the United States of America.

2. Promoting the voice and values of the Kingdom and people of Buganda.

3. Promoting African cultural values within Uganda, the African region and globally.

4. Improving socio-economic development through education, health and economic empowerment initiatives for youth, children and women.

I am grateful to Dr Carolyn Njuki and Ms Lydia Kibedi who were very instrumental in establishing the chapter and sustaining it through the early years.

'She inspires collaboration and strives to work well with others. She also eagerly confers critical skills to her team and avails herself as a sounding board. She believes that however elevated they may be, good leaders never lose sight of the bottom. In other words, they stay on top of things but keep track with their team. She, however, does not micromanage even as she keeps close tabs of the happenings at every level of the organisation'.

—Elizabeth Lwanga (Governance Board Member
Nnabagereka Development Foundation)

I am extremely proud to have served, for six years, on the board of the Nnabagereka Development Foundation an organisation whose prize has been its focus on women, children and the culture of Buganda. To this day, I remain a committed devotee to the preservation of the important cultural heritage of the Buganda Kingdom. I am thrilled to see the results of Nnaabagereka's hard work for the less fortunate.

—Jameel Verjee (Governance Board
Nnabagereka Development Foundation)

## EKISAAKAATE (Enclosure)

The Baganda cherish and celebrate their cultural heritage. However, we have had considerable challenges trying to navigate the constant pushback from Westernisation or modernisation. We live in a Euro-centric world where native African culture has for a long time been disparaged by both the West and the Africans themselves. There seems to be a pervasive imperialistic order which rates us by how well we speak and express ourselves in English; and how well we adapt to the English culture, manners and ways of life. Hence the challenging question: How do we embrace modernisation in this fast-changing world, without losing our cherished, enduring, deeply held traditions and culture?

There has always been a need to separate positive cultural traditions from negative ones. Positive traditions build strong and healthy foundations for children; build families that grow, stay and work together; encourage communal support which builds unity, shapes character, and creates a sense of belonging. These positive aspects of culture work to counteract the negative cultural norms and harmful practises that undermine the integrity and personhood of our people, especially women and girls.

In 2006, I was approached by the Minister of Youth in the Buganda Kingdom, Mr Kabuza Mukasa. He is a brilliant thinker and a widely knowledgeable observer of our culture and its intricacies. He proposed that we launch a children's camp called *Ekisaakaate*.

Back in the day, a select number of young boys attended rigorous training in the chief's enclosure or *ekisaakaate*. This form of education was critical to the grooming of future leaders and responsible officers. All girls were expected to be trained by their mothers and their paternal aunts.

I was interested.

We formed a team which included officials from the Buganda Ministry of Education, some of whom had been working with Kabuza on the Ekisaakaate concept, and staff members from my office to initiate the planning.

The result was an annual two-week intensive dubbed, *Ekisaakaate*; and later named *Ekisaakaate Kya Nnabagereka*. At the crack of dawn, the kids rise to drills, chores, training, work-shops, and of course games. The programme is carried out through in-class training sessions, storytelling (including fire-place sessions), debates and interactive discussions, practical sessions in domestics (home economics such as cooking and housekeeping); sports (physical exercises), fine arts and crafts, music, dance, drama, entertainment, cultural history, and sup-port for spiritual growth.

The driving objective is to equip children with needed life skills to become the productive men and women God has designed them to be and become responsible citizens who will effectively contribute to the nation's development and wellbeing.

> 'We started the Ekisaakaate, a two-week holiday camp. Our slogan is *'Laba. Yiga. Kola'*, which means, 'Look. Learn. Do'. All too often, we tend to focus on the child who doesn't know where his supper is coming from, but equally desperate is the child who doesn't know what to play with. Both groups are starved for *obun-tubulamu*: culture, guidance, and healthy community. They must learn how to make their beds, wash their clothes, and do common chores. We explain respect and talk about why women kneel to greet elders for example. Most importantly, they acquire life skills needful for proper development in this modern age'.
> —Honourable Maria Kiwanuka (Friend)

The first few years were hard.

My biggest regret was launching the programme before all the operational systems were in place. I remember coming up to the fourth annual Ekisaakaate camp in 2010. I felt we needed to have it at Gayaza Primary School. I felt the location and prestige of the school would enhance our brand and create even greater awareness. The chair and some members of the committee disagreed and insisted on having it at Katikamu SDA Senior Secondary school in Bulemezi. I was agreeable with them and noted, 'Okay, let's have it in Gayaza next year'! Unfortunately, members on the committee from my office didn't make it clear to the other members that I had agreed on Katikamu as the venue.

Next thing I get a call from the committee chair. 'We are really upset with your office because of your insistence on venue changes. We have decided to resign'. Shocked and distraught, I asked for a meeting the following morning. None of them showed up, but instead, they sent a signed resignation letter. Yes, my entire committee, with the exception of two members from my office, quit with just two months away from the event.

We were in crisis, but once again, I decided the 'show must go on'!

Without access to the files, we put together a new committee, headed by Kabuza Mukasa, which swiftly implemented the camp at Katikamu SDA SSS on schedule. The Kabaka graced the final day in honour of the closure of the annual camp. It was one of our most successful *Ekisaakaate*.

*Ekisaakaate Kya Nnabagereka* (*Ekisaakaate*) would become Nnabagereka Development Foundation's flagship programme. Today, it plays a big role in the education and development of our children by curbing the increasing moral decadence and the deterioration of social cohesion in our societies. To date, more than 30,000 children have benefited directly, with hundreds of thousands more indirectly from this programme.

Granted the tradition or ekisaakaate is as old as the Kingdom of Buganda itself—800 years old—the values imparted during the enclosure are still very much applicable to the contemporary era we find ourselves in today.

The goal of the Ekisaakaate is to nurture young girls and boys into holistic individuals, social managers and leaders who appreciate and harmonise both traditional and modern values.

The existence of the Ekisaakaate is an acknowledgement and response to the impact of recent political and social upheavals in our nation of Uganda. Like most African nations, our societies are suffering disruptions to our psycho-social makeup and moral fabric. I strongly believe that rebuilding our nation will entail a revival of our cultural values and unique heritage.

This programme's benefits cut across regional, race and tribal borders and is attended by boys and girls between the ages of six and eighteen. Although the programme is written from a Kiganda perspective with its cultural norms, Ekisaakaate is not created exclusively for Baganda. The values we teach transcend tribe and origins, because it is customisable to suit a particular group's needs. The curriculum creates, equips and arms future leaders with the competencies essential for transgenerational leadership.

Ekisaakaate is fast becoming a critical, credible tool for the implementation of ethics and values in our country. It is my wish that this programme be implemented throughout the world to inculcate dynamic cultural values and societal transformation.

'Her seminal achievement for sure has been the Ekisaakaate. It is so gratifying to see her courageously championing the importance of cultural values and norms in today's ever-shifting globalised world. She seems to be able to synthesise practical solutions to the daily problems ordinary people of Buganda face, while working to deepen their love and appreciation for their rich culture and heritage'.
—Dr Veronica Nakibule Kalema (Friend)

The need for values is universal, which is why we attract participants from other regions of the country, and indeed East Africa. It is gratifying to see parents from the diaspora sending kids to us.

'It is working, and not just for children from Uganda, but from Tanzania, Kenya, Zimbabwe, and beyond. We have taken the camp to England, Canada and South Africa. We hear stories of troubled kids whose lives have been completely turned around because of this amazing programme. One kid said, "I've learnt that my bad behaviour reflects not just on myself, but on my family and my community". A mother said, "Thank you very much. He is finally behaving like a civil human being"'!
—Honourable Maria Kiwanuka (Friend)

Ekisaakaate recognises culture and its perpetual evolution. Indeed, there are certain aspects of tradition that must give way to new or modernism. It is perfectly okay to challenge cultural or established norms and to determine their relevance or compatibility with conventions. Being on the cusp of change in our nation, we remain vigilant and courageous as we instruct, train and mentor our next generation.

'We have actively contributed to a revival of a cultural voice through promoting traditional values, norms, and practises. The Ekisaakaate Kya Nnaabagereka has directly equipped tens of thousands of young girls and boys (and millions more indirectly) with lifelong skills'.
–Dr Jeff Sebuyira, NDF Board Chairperson

'She has done such a tremendous job by choosing not to stay behind the palace gates, but to engage with her people. Programmes like Ekisaakaate continue to showcase her big heart. She is a formidable force for change and development in our Kingdom and indeed the entire nation'.
–Robinah Nakamate Kyazze (Aunt)

## OBUNTUBULAMU

'The Baganda have always had an inherent call to serve each other. We looked out for each other even when there was no quid pro quo. We call it *obuntubulamu*. In fact, almost every other tribal group in Africa has a similar word. We have been able to isolate over fifty distinct traits within *obuntubulamu*. Our people care, help, defend, and support one another just because it is the right thing to do. Their child is mine. Their home is mine. His or her mother was my mother. *Obuntubulamu* helped us do community. For example, my father had a 2-day, 80-mile walk to school twice a year. At the end of a day's trek, he would just walk into any house, and with open arms they fed him, got him water to shower, and housed him for the night. They didn't need to know him or require permission from his parents—that is *obuntubulamu*'.

—Judy Kamanyi (Trustee Nnabagereka
Development Foundation)

The Foundation has aligned its Ekisaakaate curriculum with the concept of *Obuntubulamu/Ubuntu*. As earlier discussed, in Buganda qualities of civility were summarised as *Obuntubulamu*. An article by Mikael Karlström titled, 'Imagining Democracy: Political Culture and Democratization in Buganda' (*Africa: Journal of the International African Institute,* Vol. 66, No. 4, p. 485-505), defines *obuntubulamu* as an expression of 'healthy humanness... a crucial term of public morality, connoting the possession of courtesy, compassion, good breeding [and] culture'. Karlström goes on to clarify that it is 'less a politico-demographic category than an ethical and civil ideal...which combines the senses of good governance and collective advancement on the level of polity with an emphasis on morality and "good manners" at the level of individual conduct'.

'In October 2019 in Accra, Ghana, the Queen of Buganda (the Nnaabagereka) took centre stage at the Global Landscape Forum (GLF) as the keynote speaker. Speaking about her culture, its connection to the African landscape, the role of youth and women

in environment issues—the world was in awe and captivated. She emphasised the role nature in cultural norms such as clans, food systems, importance of wetlands, why agroecology is not new to the Baganda people and the power of Obuntubulamu (a similar principle to Ubuntu). She delivered her message to a captivated live and virtual audience, for some it was the first time they engaged with an African Royal and understanding that our cultures have always been a natural connection to environment matters. I am in awe of her Foundations work—The Nnabagereka Foundation. At the core of the foundations work is engagement of young people and instilling the core values of Obuntubulamu. While the world has been busy preaching about the importance of youth engagement—the Nnaabageraka has been a pioneer for years advancing this in her community and beyond.'
—Dr. Musonda Mumba, Secretary General Ramsar
Convention on Wetlands Gland, Switzerland

Without a doubt, *obuntubulamu* is the mother of all virtues. It is one of the defining philosophical differences between our culture and many others. For instance, the Baganda interchangeably and randomly use the phrases *bambi* and *munange* (meaning 'dearest' and 'beloved') in their conversations. Why? It's because of *obuntubulamu*. As a people, we espouse kindness and compassion. In fact, some have mistaken this for passivity or weakness. On the contrary, we are a strong, yet highly empathetic people. This combination is critical to societal buoyancy. It is our firm belief that equipped with *obuntubulamu*, our kids can face any challenge thrown at them.

'Lady Sylvia has a character filled with authenticity, integrity and generosity. These qualities are evident in the successful programmes she has implemented through her charities like the Nnabagereka Foundation. The promotion of the Buganda culture in the diaspora, and accompanying activities like the Ekisaakaate, an event my daughter attended, is further testimony to her commitment and hard work. Her temperament indeed complements her as regal'.

–Joyce Kisubi-Muyanja (Friend)

Since there are a myriad of values which fall under the *Obuntubulamu* umbrella, the Foundation has pinpointed fourteen values which all complement the Foundation's achievements at the community and grass roots levels. Not necessarily in order of importance, they are:

1. Ensonyi (Sense of shame)
2. Okwewaayo (Selflessness)
3. Amazima (Honesty)
4. Okufa ku munno (Empathy)
5. Bulungi bwansi (Civic engagement)
6. Okweyimirizaawo (Self-Reliance)
7. Obuvunanyizibwa (Responsibility)
8. Obweerufu (Transparency)
9. Obwesimbu (Integrity)
10. Obugunjufu (Civility)
11. Obwetowaze (Humility)

12. Obuyonjo (Cleanliness/Hygiene)

13. Obwenkanya (Justice)

14. Obukulembeze (Proactive leadership)

The Foundation is drawing on the ancient African philosophy of *ubuntu* (humanity in action) with a distinctively Kiganda twist through *obuntubulamu*, and using that as a tool for social transformation within the central region of Uganda and eventually in the whole country.

It's interesting and important to note that the values (and more) espoused in *Obuntubulamu* are evidenced in just about every prominent culture on the planet, the only difference being the language and term that is used. This shared ethic builds character and serves as a connecting thread between people from different nationalities and ethnicities. The universality of these values is what makes them appealing and more importantly, particularly applicable to intergenerational leadership. Regardless of whether one is in an urban or rural area, these values resonate with just about all reasonable people, irrespective of their station in life.

'In 2020, the UN in Uganda and The Nnabagereka Development Foundation entered a partnership with six kingdoms of Acholi, Alur, Bunyoro, Busoga to localize the SDGs under the programme "An Indigenous Approach to Achieving SDGs". Through rich consultations with the Seven participating kingdoms, it was revealed that the Buganda cultural values of Obuntubulamu were shared by and ascribed to by these Kingdoms. The adoption and internalization of the

Obuntubulamu values at the individual and community level led to behavioral change and social transformation. It became a building block to national values and identity, Harnessed the social integration and endeavors to preserve local relationships in the Ugandan society and contributed to the social transformation as aligned to the national priorities in our vision. I was pleased to learn that 'Obuntubulamu' was the key driver and the new focus of all Nnabagereka Development Foundation (NDF) programmes. The universal appeal of Obuntubulamu indicates that it can play an integral role in the search for development solutions hence the United Nations in Uganda partnership to leverage on the many indigenous cultural concepts and practices to contribute to peace and development in Uganda'.

–Rosa Malango, United Nations
Director Regional Commissions

The aforementioned fourteen values are crucial to nation building and serve to equip not only youth but adults with the skills that are integral to the ethical leadership that African nations and others desperately need. They are principles of good governance, respect, non-discrimination, participation, accountability and transparency.

'We commend the Nnaabagereka for her commitment to the revival of Obuntubulamu as one of the pathways for fostering a culture that promotes ethics, integrity, peace, and sustainable development.

The young people, and communities in general, look up to cultural and religious institutions for belonging and values. We recognize the unique position that these institutions play in shaping positive behavior in society.

In the spirit of development, the Obuntubulamu core values—resonate with Sustainable Development Goals. At the national level the Obuntubulamu is a building block for the National Development Plan which prioritizes mindset change, overall national development, the vision 2040 and governance.

Socially, the moral goal of Obuntubulamu is to achieve a normative notion of personhood demonstrated in generosity, kindness, compassion, respect, and con-cern—key behavioral tenets that are associated with the promotion of the welfare of others, that would translate to inclusion.

Furthermore, Obutubulamu principles are instructive about reconciliation, sharing, civility, responsibility, trust, reform, and rehabilitation. All these elements are central to peace and development in any commu-nity or society.

From the economic viewpoint, Obuntubulamu empha-sizes social justice, equality, and equity, based on prin-ciples such as sharing and employment for all, the acceptance that 'no-one is useless' and that 'we work as one'. This is a truly progressive approach for sustainable development.

If the values and the ethical foundation emphasized are well understood, and adopted by all, they will go a long way in delivering impactful results for social transformation.

It will be easier to address serious challenges in society today, such as corruption, violence, climate change and environmental degradation; and thereby nurture accountability, responsible citizenship, and inclusive development.

–Elsie Attafuah
Resident Representative, UNDP Uganda

In 2022, I established the Nnabagereka Nagginda Women's Fund (NNWF) to 'mother' communities in Buganda Kingdom as a complement to the work of the Office of the Nnaabagereka. While the Nnabagereka Development Foundation implements programmes and projects, the NNWF is the funding arm of the Foundation and a grant-making organisation to other entities.

The Fund is capitalising on the Kingdom's convening power to build a critical mass of men and women to raise financial resources for the consistent investment in building peaceful, progressive and self-sustaining communities. NNWF seeks to grow national philanthropy in order to systematise giving in Uganda. The target beneficiaries are children, youth and women, also called our target group.

'I am really excited about where we are going as a nation. I always say this to fellow young people: Go explore; be creative; travel and do your dream, but do not forget your culture. Don't forget your roots. Remember your rich traditional history. My mom has modeled this for me. Modern as she definitely is, she is still a cultural icon for her people. She still upholds our ancient guiding traditions which have served as a beacon of light for generations. She will always be remembered as a champion for the less privileged, particularly children. I can only imagine the future impact on these kids, ten, fifteen years from now'.

—Princess Katrina-Sarah Ssangalyambogo (Daughter)

## BURNOUT

A few months after the wedding, invitations came in from all over the place. Initially, I accepted almost every one of them. I sincerely thought I was being diligent by going to almost everything I was invited to. I did school and church events, officiated launches of non-governmental initiatives and attended women's functions.

All this was great work, besides, it was charity work. Unfortunately, I started experiencing burnout. I became somewhat scattered with all the organisations' concerns in which I was engaged. I had to cut back, and I did. I started declining many invitations. Surely I didn't have to be everywhere. I needed to focus. That decision helped me maximise my influence both in Buganda and beyond.

Over the years I have championed various causes and my efforts have been spread across organisations where I served as patron or goodwill ambassador. These included: United Nations Population Fund (UNFPA); Child Fund Uganda; Special Olympics Uganda; Programme for Accessible Health

Communication and Education (PACE); Conservation Through Public Health (CTPH); and Mama Club, an initiative for mothers living with HIV/AIDS. In addition, I was a torchbearer for the Millennium Development Goals (MDG3) to promote gender equality and women's empowerment; a lead champion for the Campaign to End Paediatric HIV/AIDS in Uganda. I was also a founding board member of the African Philanthropy Forum and an Advisory Board Member on the Global Thinkers Forum.

'Sylvia is a visionary with a pretty strong head on her shoulders. When she holds a position, she will vigourously defend it, howbeit with an open mind. She is made for this. Is it easy to an outsider to marry into any royal family, let alone one with hundreds of years or pre-existing cultural norms? Of course not. But she has been amazing. She has gingerly walked the thin line between culture and modernity. She has remained unchanged by her enormous power and influence. She is touchable, caring, and genuinely interested in everyone she comes into contact with. She will grieve, rejoice, and dream with people of any caliber, and they see it! She indeed is their mother, the Nnaabagereka'!

—Mary Weeks Kironde (Friend)

'Sylvia has a good head on her shoulders. She has done a lot to promote culture awareness in our fast-changing, indigenous societies. Churches, schools, and communities big and small have been impacted by her unswerving commitment to sustainable development. As I look back, I see the invisible Hand of destiny. She was groomed for this—leadership, team building, excellent work ethic, resoluteness—all of it. This is her destiny'.

–Fred Lutalo (Cousin)

## BWINDI

'When I found out that people made gorillas sick, I was moved to immediately co-found Conservation Through Public Health. CTPH promotes biodiversity conservation by enabling people, gorillas and other wildlife to coexist through improving their health and community livelihoods in and around protected areas in Africa. At that time, I was working as the first veterinarian for Uganda Wildlife Authority. I realised that it is not possible to protect the critically endangered mountain gorillas without improving the health of their human neighbours'.

–Dr Gladys Kalema-Zikusoka

My visit to Bwindi Impenetrable National Park was a highlight of learning for me as I continued to enjoy new exciting experiences. The Bwindi Impenetrable Forest is a UNESCO World Heritage site and home to approximately half of the world's estimated population of the 720 critically endangered mountain gorillas.

Gorilla tourism contributes more than 50 percent of tourism revenue for the country. Bwindi protects over 300 robust gentle mountain gorillas. One of the greatest threats to the survival of the mountain gorillas is human-wildlife conflict due to a high population density and the ongoing existential threat of zoonotic disease.

In 2003, Dr Gladys Kalema-Zikusoka, Uganda's first gorilla veterinarian along with her husband, Lawrence and a veterinary technician Stephen Rubanga founded Conservation Through Public Health (CTPH) to promote the improvement of primary healthcare to people and animals in and around protected areas in Africa. CTPH's vision is to prevent and control disease transmission between wildlife and people. I became a patron of CTPH in May 2005, and soon after Gladys invited me to travel to Bwindi and launch the CTPH Telecentre at Buhoma, and while there, track gorillas.

In October of the same year, together with Lawrence, her mother Rhoda Kalema, Apollo Makubuya, Apollonia Mugumbya, and a few of my office staff, we took the 10-hour drive to Bwindi.

'The Nnaabagereka is a great inspiration to me. We are excited to have her as a patron of CTPH. In October 2005, she came to launch CTPH programmes at Buhoma, Bwindi. She is the first queen in the world to track the mountain gorillas. It was a momentous occasion, starting off with a graduation ceremony for candidates obtaining certificates from Makerere University's extension location at the CTPH Telecentre at Buhoma. The Nnaabagereka stayed at Volcanoes Safaris Bwindi Lodge with a nice view looking into Bwindi Impenetrable Forest'.

—Dr Gladys Kalema-Zikusoka

Trekking gorillas was an experience of a lifetime. There is nothing else I can compare it with. The journey through the thick Bwindi Impenetrable Forest was incredible! We tracked from Buhoma, walking a couple of hours through plantations, into higher greener mountains just before we entered the dense forest.

Tracking requires a reasonable amount of fitness. We made short stops a few times along the way to catch our breath as some of us hadn't been on a regular physical exercise routine which would have helped. We were accompanied by expert guides and porters who stood by to assist in case of emergencies, like if someone needed to be carried down and out of the forest. Thank God we all made it.

The walk through the impenetrable forest was tough and long through slippery valleys, hills, and swamps. After four hours, we finally caught a glimpse of a magnificent silverback gorilla and his family. Trekking through the lush, abundant thicket was captivating—but then staring into the eyes of such a giant creature so much like a human being was humbling and enthralling. Almost immediately, all the stress and fatigue of the journey felt worth the effort. It was an extraordinary feeling standing in the dense rainforest, in the company of these robust yet gentle, rare creatures.

We were asked to stay more than six metres away from the gorillas, as we watched them feed on roots, leaves and fruits. The families roam freely in the dense forest and are just like human families, made up of different personalities, ever-growing and changing, sometimes losing members to old age while gaining others through births. Fortunately, there was a new arrival, and

I was asked to name it—I chose the name *Ntuse*, which means 'I have arrived'.

> "I took the Nnaabagereka to track the Habinyanja Gorilla Group. The chief warden, John Bosco Nuwe, invited her to name a baby gorilla, who she called Ntuse, which means, "I have arrived," in commemoration of the 10-hour drive to Bwindi, and 4-hour trek to the mountain gorilla. Ntuse's mother Mukeikuru was among the eldest females in the gorilla group'.
>
> —Dr Gladys Kalema-Zikusoka

According to Dr Gladys Kalema-Zikusoka, in 2018, the mountain gorilla status changed from critically endangered to endangered because of the growth trend of this gorilla subspecies whose population has almost doubled in the past 25 years from 650 to 1063, a direct result of conservation efforts by UWA, CTPH and several partners that have led to improved veterinary care, community health and livelihoods through tourism, as well as research and law enforcement. I look forward to continuing to engage with CTPH as their patron, to ensure a brighter future for gorillas and other wildlife and the people who they share their fragile habitats with.

In 2013, on CTPH's tenth anniversary, I visited the Uganda Wildlife Education Centre and opened the exhibit for the cane rat, *omusu*, which is my clan. The centre hosts many other totems including lions, elephants and pangolins. Totems are an integral part of Buganda society. You are not allowed to kill or eat your totem, an important way of preserving nature for future generations. My daughter Princess Ssanga and I met

Hamukungu Charlie, the elephant who was rescued by CTPH community conservation animal-health workers. Hamukungu was named after the village where her rescuers came from. She was found drowning in Lake George at Queen Elizabeth National Park.

# ENTERPRISES

I am a strong advocate of the performing arts and an ardent believer that participation in various art forms, whether traditional dances or classical ballet, advances self-discipline, confidence, leadership, critical thinking and problem-solving. Dance offers a way for people to experience other cultures on an intimate level. Classical ballet, in particular, provides important lessons about aspects of dance that are beneficial to all people. Its creativity and grace is known to improve confidence, concentration, coordination, memorisation, and discipline in children and the youth.

In 2004, I started the Kampala Ballet and Modern Dance School in Nakasero, after identifying a need among parents and schools for the art. Two years later, right along with the ballet school, I opened the Café Ballet Restaurant to service students and other customers.

The history of ballet in Africa goes way back to colonial times; however, the Kampala Ballet and Modern Dance School was the first of its kind in Uganda. The school provided

pre-professional dance training adding to the already rich tradition of Ugandan dance.

The programme was met with great enthusiasm in many
schools, although not by everyone due to the nature of our
conservative culture especially when it comes to body expressions. We are very cautious of anything that we feel may compromise a woman's dignity. Some people sincerely believed that
ballet has the potential of doing so.

I travelled to Johannesburg, Pretoria, London and New
York City in search of ideas, collaborations and support for
the ballet school.

'When news of the Nnaabagereka's visit to New York
City was finally confirmed, it was difficult to know who
was more excited—the dancers, the directors, the cho-
reographers or the teachers. From ballet companies,
dance training academies, to universities and children's
schools, the New York dance community jumped to its
feet to receive the queen during her week-long, whirlwind tour in September 2005. The Nnaabagereka
effortlessly caught up with the quick pace of New York
City which she was so familiar with. In advance of her
visit, I initiated potential international partnerships
to develop the Kampala Ballet School. The queen's
visit was planned to build on these introductions and
elicit ideas and commitments to strengthen the school.
Places visited included Juilliard School, Complexions,
Paul Taylor Dance Company, New York City Ballet,
and the Alvin Ailey American Dance Theater'.

—Sara Farley (Friend)

As a result of this visit, the following year in March 2006, more than ten dance schools and companies in New York City came together in a concert to benefit the Kampala Ballet and Modern Dance School. Sara Farley and Edisa Weeks, founder and director of Delirious dance company, successfully planned and coordinated the concert. Also as a result, an annual dance programme was started between the Kampala Ballet and Modern Dance School and New York University under the leadership of Deborah Damast.

Both the ballet school and restaurant operated until 2016. Thereafter, on the same premises, on Plot 34C Kyadondo Road, Nakasero, I established Ssanga Courts, a premier-serviced apartment complex in partnership with Richard and Lydia Munyeneza under Ssanga Courts Limited. The complex is named after my daughter, Ssangalyambogo.

'The Nnaabagereka dared to embark on the revival of positive cultural norms - an uphill feat at the time. Our education, religious orientation and general modernization had castigated culture as negative and often demonic. Within the women's movement, culture was scandalized as the root cause of women's rights violations. There was a subconscious self-degradation or some self-loath of our culture as something to be discarded in order to appear civilized. Reference to culture was also perceived as condoning impunity for violence against women.

Concurrently, the women's movement was suffering from social backlash from its "equality" campaign. There was public outrage that women wanted to become men. We were castigated as combative and elitist.

Most probably, Nnaabagereka's impeccable sense of conviction that it was the right thing to do and her personal non-abrasive style enabled her cause to gain public traction. To the women's movement, she unleashed the positive reframing of our cause for a fair and equitable world in socially palatable terms, albeit she has never taken credit for it.

As a transformative result, we at FIDA-Uganda, a women's lawyers association, began to consciously amplify the positive cultural norms, mindful that to a majority of grassroots women, their first point of reference was what they knew: their culture. The resultant respect of community understanding had the ripple effect of triggering robust community dialogues, where we engaged each other as respectable human beings'.

—Dr Maria Nassali
Governance Board Vice-Chair Nnabagereka
Development Foundation & Director
Nnaabagereka Nagginda Women's Fund

# chapter 13

# EBIYIGIDDWA
## (Lessons learned)

'We live in a progressive society which is vigourously embracing globalisation with all its unintended consequences. Our core values of community and mutual respect are being eroded as individualism takes centre stage, particularly in the lives of our young people. Family has become fragmented which has resulted in a loss of societal cohesion. The Nnaabagereka's work has helped restore hope to millions. Through Ekisaakaate, she is grooming our children in critical life skills. She has championed the integration of values in humanitarianism and indigenous relief efforts by persuading organisations like the United Nations that without obuntubulamu, there cannot be fundamental improvement within our communities. I am impressed as to how she can remain sober and not get corrupted by the enormous power that her office holds. She is down-to-earth, yet meticulous and dedicated to excellence.

She has restored the centrality of women in governance and decision-making. She will be remembered as a beacon of hope and dignity to our people and Africa at large'.

–Judy Kamanyi (Friend)

## CHALLENGES

While on one hand we were making unprecedented headway, seemingly insurmountable roadblocks and challenges befell us.

Firstly, there was funding. As a result of the typically low household-income levels, very few individuals are able to fund social causes outside of their own families. That, on top of typically very limited pre-existing numbers of potential funding resources. The most obvious solution was overseas agencies. Unfortunately, there exists a negative bias from funding agencies on account of our cultural identity. The majority of these organisations deem cultural institutions as problematic and politically risky.

Secondly, competition. Cultural institutions are viewed as adversarial to indigenous mainstream establishments. They are therefore largely marginalised.

Thirdly, expectations. From day one, it felt like I was expected to meet people's high expectations, while at the same time maintaining accessibility to them. That would prove supremely challenging. Not only did I receive countless invitations to officiate at functions, but innumerable requests for personal appointments and letters asking for essential social support for things such as school fees, household help, and medical attention. In addition, there was the pressure from family members who expected personal time without consideration of the enormous demands of my office and status. Demands like security, time pressure, and protocol determined my availability.

## COPING

Eventually, I found my rhythm. I learnt to cope with my load. And here is how:

- I found courage to persevere regardless of the challenges. None of this was a cakewalk. I have had to push through even on the darkest of days, while drawing support from friends and close associates.

- I chose to stay focused on my objective in spite of the numerous distractions, I was able to resist negativity and chose to replace it with positivity and purposeful thinking.

- I harnessed tested knowledge and experience of elders. Although not all of them were highly educated, they were rich in critical life experiences and wisdom.

- I consulted with technical experts. After three decades of destruction and upheavals, the Kingdom had no funds to hire expertise. However, many of them were willing and able to offer their time and resources to contribute to the restoration of the glory of Buganda Kingdom. Even today, many people still offer their services free of charge to the Kingdom. They do this to give back to a Kingdom which has served as a melting pot for the entire country.

- I leaned into my life experiences over the years. These include my studies at primary and secondary schools in Uganda, to American universities, my engagement in student activism, job experiences with the United Nations and other organisations and corporations. All these seasons contributed to preparing me for my current role as Nnaabagereka. My communication and public relations background was particularly helpful in training me to relate to people internally and externally. Clear and effective communication has been perhaps the most important of all life skills without which professional and personal relationships could have never been held together. It has helped me win over people.

- The passion to see others do well and or do better; being sympathetic to others plight and the desire to help them overcome hardships.

'Sylvia is genuinely interested in all of us. Every time I see her, she diligently asks concerning every one of our mutual friends. She has helped elevate needy children, women and other disadvantaged classes of people.'

—Robinah Mukasa (Friend)

- Finally, I learnt respect for self and others, as a fundamental notion in our culture, not just for creating boundaries but to accord the self-worth that every individual deserves.

'Over the years, we have shared great memories—marriages, births, deaths—which have revealed the true leader and inspiration that Sylvia truly is. She has encouraged me to never give up, and to remain unflinchingly optimistic. I have watched her exhibit one of her greatest strengths—to keep on going even when everything around seems to be falling apart. There is way more to be accomplished by this super special person, Sylvia Nagginda Luswata Mutebi. Her legacy has just begun'.

–Lydia Kibedi (Friend)

## LESSONS

So, what have I learnt? Let me break it down in nugget form.

1. Concerning patience: I have learnt to keep steady, persistent, and resilient. I have learnt to recognise when impatience is creeping in, trying to make things happen overnight instead of focusing on the cause ahead of me.

2. Concerning titles: The simple English equivalent for the Nnaabagereka is 'queen', so from the get-go, I was expected to live, walk, talk, act and work as a queen in the British sense of the word, since

Uganda was a British colony. It's what we know. Simply put, the Nnaabagereka's role was a cluster of assumed duties and responsibilities. But then, the tide blew me into a totally different direction. This was nothing like the British monarch, and certainly different from the old days of my father-in-law's reign. Titles shouldn't define one's life or function. I believe that it's what you chose to do with whatever title you hold that really matters.

'It is so refreshing to see how well Sylvia has done for the people in her country. Rave reviews of her accomplishments on multiple platforms around the world, including UNAIDS in Geneva, clearly show that she is one of the most respected people in Uganda. 'Thinking back, to me Sylvia has always been a queen! The title hasn't changed her character, she's still true to herself and her friends. I'm so proud to be able to say that she's a friend. I feel blessed to have met her'.

—Virginie Mongonou (Friend)

3. Concerning team: As the Foundation grew, I realised that my vision required special attention to those assigned to work with me. I had to put the interests of others at the forefront of my agenda. Working for them automatically meant working for me. When they benefited, I did too. Selfishly excluding them would be set up to my own failure. I also had to identify people who genuinely believed in the cause and surrounded myself with those who knew more than I did for guidance.

The younger generation can benefit so much from the experiences and wisdom of our predecessors.

4. Concerning courage: One indispensable trait of all success is courage. In my case, I have needed courage to dare to be and do different. Be ready to take the often-dreaded first steps ahead of the line to challenge the status quo. Believe in a better, yet unknown future and hope that your efforts today will yield a better tomorrow. With foresight and continued commitment, we all can meet the challenges at hand.

5. Concerning work: Find something that interests you and go after it. There is no shortcut to direct personal engagement and commitment to the work at hand. A good leader is constantly aware of what's happening in their organisation at all levels. That doesn't mean they micromanage systems, but that they are always aware of what's going on. Be accessible by keeping open lines of communication. Remember that people want to feel wanted and respected. Don't be afraid to share important contacts and leads. Always be civil even as you remain assertive. Strive to collaborate and work well with your team as you inspire teamwork among the team.

6. Concerning integrity: Integrity can be simply defined as who you are when no one is watching. Truly successful people are people of principle. They have high levels of transparency and accountability. Your character will guard your reputation, which is often a leader's most valuable commodity.

'Throughout the years, she has remained the same—a loyal person who honours relationships, friendships and family. She treats everyone equally, sometimes even better than they deserve. When I am with her, she makes me feel like I am the most important person ever. That is her gift. I am convinced that she will always be remembered as a caring, generous heart'.

—Ruth Nabeta (Friend)

7. Concerning service: Serve to serve; serve the people so that they in turn will gladly serve. When you provide good and beneficial service, you will reap profit, but even more, respect and credibility.

'Though she stands for the continuity and tradition of the Buganda institution, since becoming queen she has broken centuries-old royal tradition by redefining what it means to be the Nnaabagereka of Buganda. This has not come without tremendous challenges which she has faced with discipline, dignity and grace. Indeed, there have been some deeply testing times. And as expected perhaps, her enemies would wish to undermine her work, but her faith, character and resilience help her remain strong and focused on what she wants to achieve for Buganda and Uganda. She consults widely and she remains teachable. Consequently, she has become a role model for many young girls and boys all over the world'.

—The Venerable Archdeacon
Emeritus Prince Daniel Kajumba

'I knew then as I know now that her desire has always been to care for people. There is no other place to effectively do this than where she is now as queen of our Kingdom. I thank her for being herself: for being, kind, gentle, accepting, positive. Not even the title of Nnaabagereka or the Crown has changed her. She's my big sister, an extraordinary person and I thank her for impacting my life'.

—Elsie Mukasa-Kalebu (Friend)


# PROVIDENCE

As I look back at my journey, I see God's guiding hand evidenced through the different seasons within it. Here are a few examples:

## 1. Education

A master's degree in corporate communication, along with my intense work experience in public relations helped train me to relate with people. I learnt how to communicate information accurately and effectively—a vital life skill which is arguably most important of all. Along with good communication came the critical organisational skills that aided in winning people over. It is this potent combination of my traditional upbringing in a chief's home and my Western education and experiences that have helped prepare me for this position.

## 2. Role Models

Another key factor has been the role models along my winding journey. My well-to-do, comfortable grandparents' home also attracted needy and very poor people. I grew up seeing my grandparents caring and providing for these needy people with what I can only describe as God's bountiful love. By watching them, I learnt empathy and charity. Furthermore, my mother inspired me to work hard and to reach out for the best to succeed.

> 'Throughout the years, she has remained the same—a loyal person who honours relationships, friendships and family. She treats everyone equally, sometimes even better than they deserve. When I am with her, she makes me feel like I am the most important person ever. That is her gift. I am convinced that she will always be remembered as a caring, generous heart'.
>
> —Ruth Nabeta (Friend)

### 3. God's Grace

My success can best be summed up in one phrase—the grace of God. It is in Him that I fully trust and firmly believe. Being spiritually grounded feeds my soul and sustains my body and mind. Believing in a God-ordained future, and hoping that our energies of today will yield a better tomorrow keeps me motivated in the face of life's harsh realities. Each day, I pray for foresight and continued commitment to enable me to meet the challenges ahead.

### 4. Gratitude

I never take any of this for granted. I am grateful for the opportunity that I have been given to serve as the Nnaabagereka. It is not about the title or position, but what am able to do with it. My constant prayer is that what I do with it will go a long way in making a difference to the wellbeing of my fellow Ugandans and beyond.

'Queen Sylvia is intelligent, classy, humble, respectful, kind with an affable demeanor. She's a good listener and stands by her friends with unflinching loyalty. Even my children consider her a safe confidant. She loves God and genuinely prays for those in need around her and beyond. She is a very special woman. I guess that is the reason why God chose her to be our queen'.

—Sarah Kiyingi-Kaweesa (Cousin)

'Her gracious nature, selflessness and sense of humour have not changed, in spite of her elevation as Her Royal Highness the Queen. She continues to bring credibility, respect and grace to Buganda and indeed the whole country. She is a role model to young girls and women everywhere'.

—Deborah Lukwago Alibu (Friend)

## 5. Goodwill

I attribute my success to the environment in which I carry out my assignment. As wife of the Kabaka, the Nnaabagereka is inexorably positioned to influence. She leverages the people's loyalty and allegiance to the monarchy to motivate them to a mutually desired end. From time immemorial, the Baganda have identified the Kabaka as a source of basic identity, inspiration, and influence. They hold him in high esteem as he commands great respect and authority, even beyond the Kingdom.

'I couldn't be prouder of her for everything she has done. She has always been a voice to the voiceless. She has inspired me to view my own journey as preparation for something much bigger than me. Can I leverage my corporate experience in the banking sector to influence my generation? Absolutely! While it is a fact that without culture, we are nothing; and that some cultural elements must not change—dress, the dances, the language, virtues. Sylvia is showing how to courageously re-examine culture through a modern lens. Her work with NDF aims to expose the diaspora to this extremely exciting perspective. The NDF USA chapter plans to take a more prominent role in the future of the whole organisation'.

—Monique Codjoe (Sister)

## LOVE THY NEIGHBOUR

My tenure and experience at the United Nations gave me a deeper appreciation for diversity. I believe that a basic appreciation for multiculturalism and ethnicity is critical to the development of children and young people in this 21st century melting pot. More than ever, the world has shrunk. We are no longer seen as the so-called 'dark continent' isolated from the rest of the world. Tolerance and diversity are essential, but without an appreciation for who we are, how can we expect to reach out and understand our neighbours?

When kids appreciate their uniqueness, they are better able to reach out beyond themselves, beyond their own tribes, race and culture. At the *Ekisaakaate*, we gather participants from many tribes and nationalities. We are a force for unity and diversity.

> 'Initially, it was hard getting my bearings around the culture. It is so different from how I was raised here in New York. I felt disadvantaged for not feeling "Ugandan" enough. To make matters worse, I was expected to know stuff. I was the queen's close relative. Did I like traditions like kneeling before my own sister? Not really, but I totally appreciated them. I learnt that I didn't really have to like it. It was an honour to do culture. Eventually, I grew to absolutely love it. I feel terrible for some of my friends who don't know where they are from. I don't have to take a DNA test to know that I am a Muganda from Uganda'.
>
> —Monique Codjoe (Sister)

I should point out that it is God who created us so differently. The Bible says, *'Thank you for making me so wonderfully complex. Your workmanship is marvelous—how well I know it'!* (Psalm 139:14).

Yes, we are complex—black, brown, red, white, or tall, short, and so on. Celebrating our culture and uniqueness doesn't mean segregation. It is almost an act of worship to God.

It is written: *'". . .Love your neighbor as yourself." No other commandment is greater than these'* (Mark 12:31). In as much as I believe in making a strong showing through the Foundation, I also desire that the organisation can stand, and in fact thrive without me. I am a strong believer in legacy. Whatever we build should outlast us. This is a driving philosophy with everything I do.

Like the British band Queen, sang: 'The show must go on'! The Foundation is not about me. It is bigger than me!

My greatest joy comes from my contribution to the betterment for our people. Hopefully, I have made the title more appealing and enhanced its meaning and outlook—believing in a great future and hoping that my energies of today will yield a better tomorrow.

My journey is a work in progress. I urge all people to join me in this voyage as we apply ourselves to the furtherance of a better tomorrow for every one of us, and the generations ahead. To my fellow traditional and cultural leaders in Uganda and elsewhere in Africa, let's continue to explore the endless opportunities to serve our people. Let's revive positive traditional practises that provide for gender equality, while also guaranteeing our women lives of dignity.

My prayer:

Lord, You have blessed me to be a blessing to others and have uniquely placed me to be the Nnaabagereka of Buganda for such a time as this. Show me how to use the position and gifts that You have given me for Your glory. Transform me into a person of greatness and let me not be afraid of losing my life. Help me to always be obedient to You, no matter the cost. In the name of Jesus, amen!

(Adapted from a prayer in Dr Michelle Corral's book, *Through the Eyes of Esther*)

# EPILOGUE

One of my biggest fears was rejection. *What if they don't like me? What if they shun me as the Nnaabagereka?* And indeed, they very well could have. They didn't know me. Having left Uganda as a teenager to live abroad for eighteen years, I suppose their skepticism would somewhat be justified. Maybe they would assume that my Western education would make me too snobbish or too sophisticated to mingle with 'regular folk'.

Yes, it has been the favour of God. I cannot take any of this for granted. Does everyone like me? No, but overall, they recognise my place in the story of our people and this nation.

Am I driven? Absolutely, driven to contribute to the rebuilding of our Kingdom and the nation at large. I always wanted to solve some problems and contribute to the betterment of my fellow citizens, particularly those who couldn't help themselves. I never anticipated the impact. Even when significant reports started coming in, my mind refused to process any of it as personal achievements.

I remember thinking, *What are they talking about? What do these people see in me? All I do is attend some functions here or there, give an inspirational speech once in a while, and lend my status to a couple of things around the country. Yes, we do charity work to help solve some critical needs, but others do it too. What I am doing surely can't be any different.*

I'd hear their beautiful compliments, but it didn't register with me. I actually don't think it ever will. Maybe it is one of my flaws. I tend to diminish my own accomplishments.

When people—complete strangers—stop to greet me or smilingly wave from afar, their eyes tell me a different story. I figure they deserve a moment of my full attention, so I wave and smile back.

I am not some master strategist; I don't have image consultants making sure I say the right things, make strategic public appearances or media presence. All is a result of the favour of God. And as this story continues, my prayer is continued humility and gratefulness.

God is my anchor. Do I get discouraged, attacked, maligned or challenged? Yes, just like every other public figure. The difference is I have chosen to not ride it out alone. I can't keep all the balls in the air. I can't always keep all the voices of negativity at bay. But I have a seasoned Captain—our Lord Jesus Christ—who helps me navigate life's treacherous waters. I have surrounded myself with godly people who speak truth to me and pray for me.

Unfortunately, I have not always had a personal relationship with God. I remember responding to invitations for salvation early in high school, but as the years rolled on, I slipped away. I kept Him at a distance, something which I deeply regret.

If I were to advise 16-year-old Sylvia right now, I would say two things:

1. Trust God: Don't do life alone because you can't. It is much too complicated, painful, and unpredictable.

2. Be patient: Nothing worthwhile comes quickly. You will need to till hard before you harvest anything meaningful.

I hope that in some way, God has used my story to encourage, challenge or inspire you. Remember this: You also have a story. Live it! Make a difference wherever God has placed you. My prayer is that you may be the change for your community, city, tribe and country.

Love and blessings always!

# NOTE FROM THE BIOGRAPHER

'Guys, there is a reporter in New York who wants to interview Limit X for her radio show', someone announced. For a while, we'd been waiting for such opportunities that could open doors for us in the USA. Moreover, the British press had already dubbed us, 'Europe's answer to America's Boys II Men'.

As fascination with our music grew into a global frenzy, we never forgot Sylvia the enchanting Ugandan American reporter who first introduced us to our American audience. She was delightful, polite and intellectually engaging.

Years later, we heard of the budding romance between her and His Majesty King Ronald Mutebi. It was a joy when news of the royal wedding reached us while on tour. She would no longer be that obscure New York reporter, but Her Majesty Queen Sylvia Luswata, the Nnaabagereka of Buganda.

It is only by happenstance that we reconnected through my friend Prince Daniel Kajumba. When she asked to interview me to help write her story, I was elated, then anxious, especially after I learnt that she had a journalism degree. This would be unlike anything I had worked on. And indeed, it has been!

Working on this book has been a most thrilling adventure. The five-year journey has involved hundreds of hours and dozens of interviews in multiple cities and continents around the world. Experiencing the power of such a moving, real-life fairy tale is every writer's dream. I shall forever be grateful to Her Royal Highness for the honour.

What is most impressive to me is that while the rest of the world tributes her as one of Africa's most powerful queens, her family and friends know her simply as Sylvia, the extremely kind-hearted, down-to-earth, super-generous soul.

Your Royal Highness, it has been a true honour chronicling your incredible journey. I am certain that there is so much more yet for you to accomplish as you continue to fulfil your destiny. Do know that I shall be at your humble service when you and destiny shall call to write the next chapter of your unfolding story.

*Dr Dennis Sempebwa*
Biographer
sempebwa.com

# WHAT OTHERS ARE SAYING...

'I thank the Nnaabagereka for exhibiting remarkable devotion to culture and focusing on uplifting the standard of living of our people. She is an inspiration to the young generation and has demonstrated to the world that gender discrimination is no longer fashionable. Her resourcefulness and competence are a great asset to the nation'.

*H.E President Yoweri K. Museveni*
Republic of Uganda

'I salute HRH the Nnaabagereka for her persistent effort to instill good morals and proper culture norms and behaviour in our young people, even beyond the borders of Buganda'.

*First Lady Janet K. Museveni*
Republic of Uganda

'The Nnaabagereka is a very good friend of Tooro Kingdom. Our families share long histories. I believe that her era has just begun. She has tremendous responsibilities. I pray that God stays with her and continues to show her the way'.

*Princess Royal Elizabeth Bagaya*
Kingdom of Tooro

'The Nnaabagereka's work is breeding a social movement that is consequential to creating a new breed of formative ability to sustain peace and development in a world where the two are in great jeopardy'.

*Rosa Malango*
Resident Coordinator
United Nations
USA

'As Good Will Ambassador and Advocate, the work of Her Royal Highness has helped to protect the rights and improve lives of children and women at community, national, regional and international levels'.

*Dr Jotham Musinguzi*
Regional Director
Partners in Population and Development Africa
Republic of Uganda

'We commend the Nnaabagereka for her commitment to the revival of Obuntubulamu as one of the pathways for fostering a culture that promotes ethics, integrity, peace, and sustainable development'.

*Elsie Attafuah*
Resident Representative
UNDP Uganda

'I commend the Nnaabagereka for playing the role of a parent to so many children. While many parents are too busy to support their children on issues of growing up and maturation, she continues to help them prepare to be responsible citizens'.

*Honourable Jessica Alupo*
Former Minister of Education and Sports
Government of Uganda

'She has played a major role in sensitising and mobilising the general population on issues of education, health, poverty eradication and culture preservation. She is an inspiration to many people not only in Buganda but Uganda and the world at large'.

*The most Reverend Archbishop Henry Luke Orombi*
The Anglican Church
Republic of Uganda

'Her programmes, well-suited for sound moral education, reflect a mother's concern for her children. I wish her many happy years and abundant blessings from above'.

*Archbishop Emeritus Emmanuel Cardinal Wamala*
The Catholic Church
Republic of Uganda

'In the midst of political, cultural, and socio-economic difficulties, her exemplary contribution is a rare phenomenon in modern times deserving special attention'.

*Metropolitan Archbishop Jonah Lwanga*
Uganda Orthodox Church
Republic of Uganda

'It is gratifying and encouraging to see that she is in the battle-field fighting to overcome under development'.

*Sheik Shaban Ramadhan Mubaje*
Mufti of Uganda
Republic of Uganda

'Being educated, smart, motherly, and approachable has respectfully made the Nnaabagereka a humble servant to all subjects irrespective of religion, race and tribe throughout our beloved Nation'.

*The late Sheikh Sowed Zubair Kayongo*
Former Supreme Mufti
Republic of Uganda

'The Nnaabagereka has been exemplary at putting the virtue of charity into practise by caring for the marginalised. She works passionately to fulfil her vision of uplifting the standards of living for Ugandans. She is a positive role model to many people regardless of their culture, religion, and age'.

*Dr Cyprian Kizito Lwanga*
Archbishop of Kampala
The Catholic Church
Republic of Uganda

'HRH the Nnaabagereka has acted in humility empowered by the Holy Spirit to touch the hearts of those who are hurting, to reach and help the desperate, to feed the hungry, to fulfil her role as a mother to Buganda and Uganda while trusting God in all things'.

*The Right. Reverend Wilberforce Kityo Luwalira*
Bishop of the Diocese of Namirembe
The Anglican Church
Republic of Uganda

'The Nnaabagereka has visited the sickest patients in their homes and has consoled bereaved family members when their ones have died. Her foundation (NDF) demonstrates a spirit of mindfulness for less fortunate persons, which is within the Hospice Africa Uganda (HAU) ethos'.

*Hospice Africa*
Republic of Uganda

'The Nnaabagereka of Buganda has shown a true heart of a woman leader and mother who goes out of her way to meet the needs of her people. I commend Her Royal Highness for choosing not to sit back and watch Ugandans go through struggles, but instead she used her position to be part of the struggle'.

*Professor Apollo R. Nsibambi*
Former Prime Minister
Republic of Uganda

# INDEX OF NAMES

# PICTURES

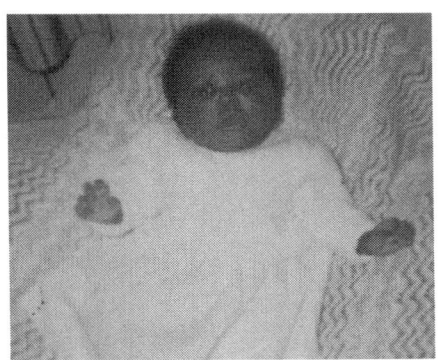

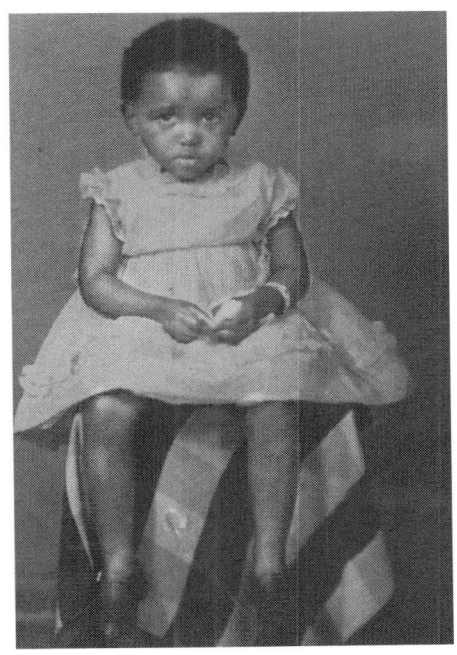

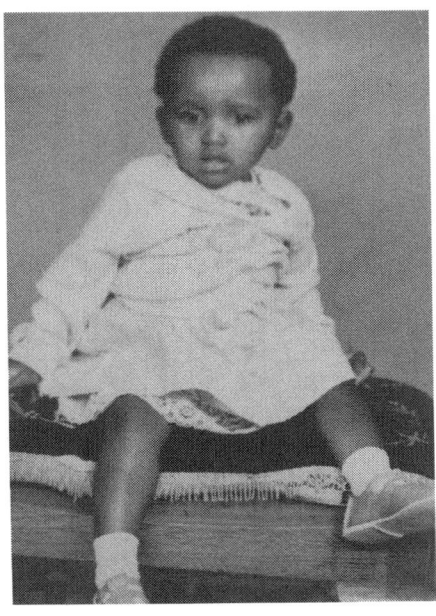

The baby Sylvia Nagginda Luswata

Young Sylvia with Grandpa Sebugwawo
and Aunt Ssenga Cate Bamundaga

My grandmother – Maama

Olivia, Sylvia, Eddie, and Rosel at Jajja's house at Nkumba

Grandmother – Maama

Grandpa Omutaka Nelson Sebugwawo –
Buganda Kingdom Chief

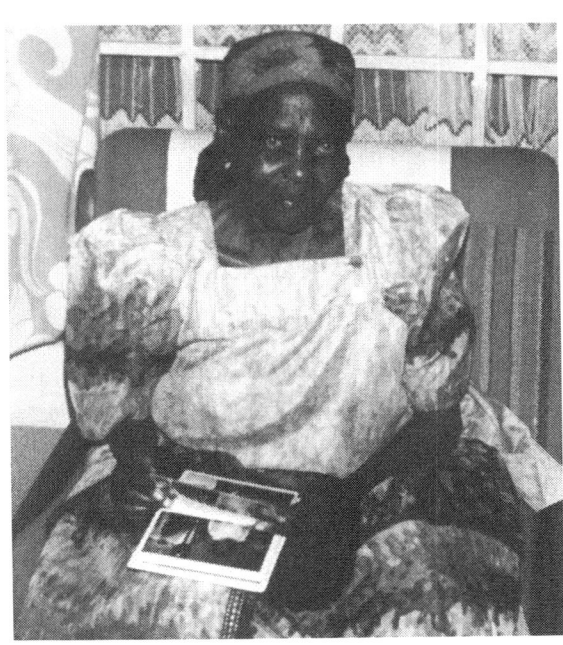

Great grandma Sarah Namyenya –
Jajja we Manyangwa

My daddy and Kabaka at Kireka Palace

My daddy with his older brother Uncle Dan Sebugwawo

My grandfather and father

Stone on taata-grandpa's house
where Sylvia grew up in at Nkumba

Taata my Grandpa house Sylvia grew up in at Nkumba

Jajja Ma and Sylvia

Kabaka's mother –
Kabejja Sarah Nalule

Kabaka Fred Mutesa II with my grandfather,
the young Nelson Sebugwawo

Maternal grandparents – George Musoke and my Grandma

Kabaka & Nnaabagereka Wedding

Kabaka & Nnaabagereka Wedding

Kabaka & Nnaabagereka – Kanzu Gomesi Portrait

Wedding: the Groom, the Bride, and Archibishop Nkoyoyo

Wedding Day Aug 27th 1999
The bride and the groom outside the church, after the service

Wedding: the President, the First Lady, Tooro,
the King, the Princes and the Princess

Wedding Party

Sylvia with her mum Rebecca

Sylvia – teenager in Secondary school

Sylvia at the NYU Graduation

Dad Maxwell and Mum Rebecca

Sylvia with her mum Rebecca

The Luswata Family with the grankids

Sylvia with her brother Nelson Luswata

Dad Luswata, mummy Edith, and Sylvia

Sylvia with siblings, Rueben and Monique

Rueben and Sylvia

Monique and Sylvia

Kabaka Family – the young Junju, Vicky, Joan, and the baby Ssanga

Kabaka Mutebi Family Portrait

Mummy with the girls Joan, Vicky, and Ssanga

Junju, Vicky, Joan, Ssanga, and Richard

Jade Nakato

Jasmine Babirye

Jade and Jasmine – 10 years old

Sylvia, Sarah, Junju, Kss, Joan, and Vicky

Children – Junju, Joan & Vicky

Mummy Rebecca – reading newspaper
after the Okufumba function

My Aunt Ssenga Cate Bamundaga

Fred Lutalo with Grandpa

HRH Queen Sylvia Nagginda Luswata

Sylvia with Cate Nabankema Bwete

On Empowering women – a light moment in the communities

At the Kampala School for the Physically Handicapped

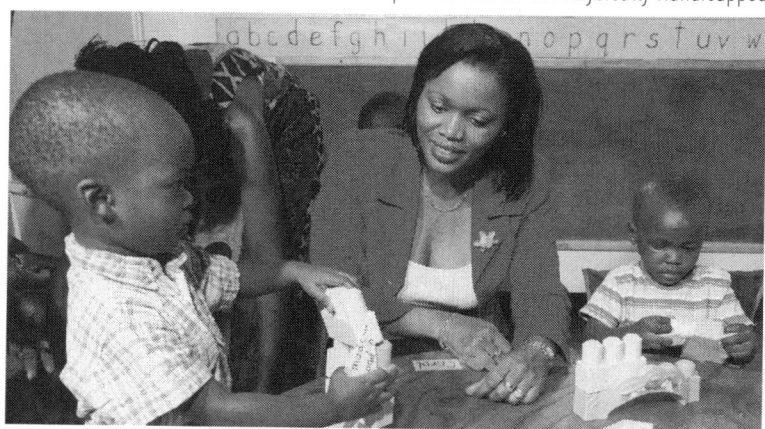

With children at the Sanyu babies home

At a Speaking Engagement

In the Bwindi Impenetratable Forest

With Kabaka at Bulange

Kabaka Nnabagereka with King Asantehene Osi TuTu – Ghana

# CLIPPINGS

## UPC demands probe of militias

# Nnabagereka takes Ekisaakate to UK

Nnabagereka with some of the Ekisaakate participants in the UK last Saturday

# Nnabagereka in UK for cultural education

Meeting. The Nnabagereka of Buganda, Ms Sylvia Nagginda (left), greets Mr Magwaja Kisaga in Manchester, United Kingdom, yesterday.

309

MONDAY, JUNE 22, 2016 3

## national

**Daily Monitor**
www.monitor.co.ug

# Nabagereka: Read books to get out of poverty

**Partnership.** Aristoc donates books worth millions of shillings to the Nnabagereka Development Foundation.

STEPHEN WANDERA
wguma@gmmonimedia.com

KAMPALA. Youth must embrace a reading culture especially of books on how to become successful entrepreneurs, if they to break vicious cycle of poverty, the Nnabagereka of Buganda Sylvia Nnaginda has said.

"Research shows that Ugandans have a poor reading culture. I encourage children to explore the pleasure of books and reading and parents to provide them with the opportunity to always have a book of their own to read," she said at the opening of Aristoc Bookstore at Acacia Mall on Friday.

"Bookstores are often the only readily available source of complementary information needed by people for personal, family and job related purpose. Our community's economy benefits when business people use bookstore resources to make wise business decisions, empses see it to improve skills, and the deprived use it to help break the cycle of poverty."

**Love for reading**

The Nnabagereka, who hailed Margaret Katende the proprietor of the bookstore, also said Aristoc

Bookstore is a cornerstone of healthy community that gives people the opportunity to be informed, educated, entertained, research, experience new ideas and inspiration.

"I believe passionately in encouraging a love of reading in young people of all ages. Reading is exciting and fun.

There is nothing quite like the thrill of opening a book and being drawn into another world to meet new people and discover their stories. The power of a gripping story and intriguing character is immense. It transports us into different and sometimes strange worlds, and helps us to understand why people behave as they do, for a moment we experience other people' journeys and livelihoods. It is a true voyage of discovery that broaden and stimulate our minds."

John Katende, Aristoc director announced a donation of books worth Shs1 million to Nnabagereka's Development Foundation.

Ms Katende and the Nnabagereka adds for a sculpture at the newly opened Aristoc Bookstore. PHOTO BY STEPHEN WANDERA

FEBRUARY ... 2014 5

**Sunday Monitor**
www.monitor.co.ug

**Together. Buganda, Ford Foundation partner for development**

The queen of Buganda Sylvia Nnaginda (2nd L) with Ford Foundation vice president Hilary Pennington (C) at Bulange Mengo during the launch of the 2014 – 2019 strategic plan on Friday. Ms Pennington pledged of $100,000 (about Shs270 million) towards the plan. PHOTO BY STEPHEN WANDERA

**32** NEW VISION, Wednesday, March 13, 2019

LIFESTYLE

# Celebrating women Rotary in style

By Denis Nsubuga

Women at Rotary annual dinner held at Kampala Serena Hotel last Saturday were a definition of elegance and glam.

Organised by the Rotary Club of Kampala Naalya, the evening saw the over 300 Rotarians guests dine and dine, as they swayed to to Victoria Hall.

Inside the ballroom, the décor was delicate and Froga Band serenaded the guests.

Graced by Nnabagereka Sylvia Nagginda, the talk of the evening revolved around women's issues and achievements.

The dinner was also intended to raise funds to support the Information and Communication Technology facilities at Akwanga Hills Secondary School in Agago district.

To kick off discourse were insightful speeches from Rotary District 9211 governor, Shamira Rhut, and Kenyan lawyer Carol Musyoka, which triggered thought about the image of women in an African society.

Comparisons with their male counterparts on political representation and leadership were drawn. Achievements of gender equity in countries like Uganda where 54% of the population in Parliament is female, were celebrated.

Rotary District 9211 is made up of Tanzania and Uganda.

As guests sipped on endlessly flowing drinks, the evening went into a panel discussion.

The panelists were former minister Victoria Ssekitoleko, architect Phyllis Ssemoga, gender rights activist

workplaces.

But, notably, like Sekimoko park, and many guess seemed to concur, "education of girls is the most important element in achieving the much-needed gender balance."

**Awards**

One of the major highlights was the Women in Rotary Awards 2019. The biggest winners of the night were Ruth Kavuma of Forum for African Women Educationists Uganda (FAWEU), leadership, Vivian Kityo of Wakiso Ministries, community service, and Gerry Opoka of Soul Finest Limited, innovation.

The icing on the cake was the last speech by Nagginda who called on Rotarians to empower the youth to become agents of transformation.

Here presided a sumptuous

*Nnabagereka (third-left) cutting cake with Rotary Club members.* Photos by Denis Nsubuga

*Post Bank staff who pledged to support the Nnabagereka Foundation*

---

MONDAY, JANUARY 19, 2015 **3**

**Daily Monitor**
www.monitor.co.ug

## national

# First Lady praises Nnabagereka for promoting culture

BY JOSEPH KATO

KAMPALA. First Lady Janet Museveni has commended the Nnabagereka of Buganda, Sylvia Nagginda, for promoting culture through Ekisaakaate, the royal enclosure cultural bold learning that plays a key role in helping the children connect the dots between the realities of the world we live in.

Ms Museveni, who was the guest speaker at the climax of this holiday's camp at St Lawrence Crhuge High School Crown City Campus in Mpigi District at the weekend, took note of Nnabagereka's ingenuity and encouraged her to continue with the "excellent work" done by her foundation.

"I would like to congratulate the Nnabagereka of Buganda for the foresight and determination to make a difference in the lives of the children of this nation," Ms Museveni said, adding: "My dear sister and friend, the importance of work being done by this foundation is demonstrated by the enthusiasm in which parents have been enrolling their children for this holiday program."

Ms Museveni, who is also the minister for Karamoja Affairs, said: "Loss of culture is as bad as losing your identity" and encouraged students to always observe their culture.

She said culture promotes self-esteem. The camp was attended by more than 400 pupils and students from the different regions of the country. To a great extent, she said, "loss of culture is like loss of your own identity."

She appealed to the participants to identify their culture first thus the rest would follow.

"Having identity is essential, health and contributes a great deal for personal self-esteem among students. Besides, it is the way to ground patriotism and nationalism," she added.

Ms Museveni discouraged a "disturbing trend"

of children engaging in sexual activities that contributing to premature motherhood.

"This trend can be directly linked to poor upbringing where children are not taught, guided and directed by their parents. It is the role of parents to pass the necessary value to their children" she said.

The Nnabagereka urged parents to befriend their children saying some children fear to tell

parents the challenges they face because of being rude and strict. "These children, tell us a lot of things when they are here. They fear to discuss such issues to you because you're so strict and rude. Make them your friends it will help you know what they are facing," she said.

The students who talked to Daily Monitor said they had learnt a lot and that the camp changed their lives for the better.

*Ekisaakaate participants display food wrapped in banana leaves locally known as luwombo at St Lawrence Citizens High School Crown City Campus in Mpigi District at the weekend.* PHOTO BY STEPHEN WANDERA/DAILY

DAILY MONITOR THURSDAY, JUNE 5, 2020

# Conserving biodiversity is crucial

As the world marks the World Environment Day (WED) today under a Covid-19 infected world, it is evident how our food systems have been the saving grace for many communities. This pandemic has also shown us the importance nutritious food systems for human well-being. As the theme of the WED stands: "Time for Nature"- biodiverse agroecological food systems have been central to life in Buganda Kingdom and other parts of Uganda.

WED comes in the heels of the Global Nutrition Report 2020 that was launched online mid-May by the Food and Agriculture Organisation of the UN. The importance of having a balanced and nutritious diet emanates from good food sources that come from landscapes with healthy soils and landscapes.

Uganda is blessed with agroclimatic conditions that make the landscape suitable for growing vegetables. Most of these are traditional vegetables that grow mostly during the rainy season and many communities have been dependent on them for hundreds of years. These traditional vegetables have been credited for high nutritional value providing people with the much needed micronutrients, ascorbic acid and mostly vitamins A and C and dietary fiber. These traditional vegetables grow mostly around forests and wetland systems near cultivated areas.

Scientific findings have shown that Vitamin A, for example, is important for children's development and as such, should be a part of their diet and that of lactating mothers. Examples of these traditional vegetables that have formed part of the Luganda culture include *Ensuga* (Solanum nigrum), *Ejjobyo* (Gynandropsis gynandra), *Ttimba* (Colocasia esculenta) to mention but a few. The tra-

> Women play a pivotal role in agroecological food systems.

**Sylvia Nagginda**
**Food system**

ditional vegetables have not only been sources of food, but also historically used to source products such as dyes, coffee substitutes, ornamentals and many others.

The Kingdom of Buganda and the rest of the country relies heavily on agroecological and agriculture most of which is subsistence. Covid-19 has also demonstrated how a compromised immunity could prove deadly.

We, as a kingdom, also strongly believe that biodiversity conservation is critical to maintaining ecosystem services that support agriculture. Practiced for hundreds of years, in Buganda, agroecological and traditional practices have left buffer zones or uncultivated sections that are adjacent to a forest or wetland ecosystem. With this, we have seen increase in bees and other biodiversity necessary for pollination at the same time other wildlife that support pest control.

Buganda calls for recognition that our food systems are dependent mainly on family farms most of which are managed and tilled by women. As the UN Decade on Family Farming comes into effect - it also coincides

with the in-coming UN Decade on Ecosystem Restoration (2021-2030) that calls for the conservation of the agroecological systems that we have. Unfortunately many ecosystems – forests, wetlands and agroecological zones – have been degraded and as such compromising the very food systems we depend on. This is further compounded by climate change that impacts the most vulnerable, particularly women. A loss of biodiversity particularly the traditional vegetables, could not only result in the impairment of ecological, but also cultural functions. Cultural uses of those vegetables are associated to traditional ceremonies and beliefs such as weddings, births and receiving of visitors.

Our kingdom acknowledges the pivotal role women play in agroecological food systems. It also recognises the challenges and burden that climate change places women and children. Unfortunately, biodiversity loss has implications for local livelihoods, especially women whose lives are impacted the most. Evidence points to effects such as land conversion, droughts, floods, disease have resulted in the loss of some of these traditional vegetables. The recent flooding dynamic around the Lake Victoria demonstrates how the impact of climate change continue to affect vulnerable communities. As the Sustainable Development Goals clearly stipulate, we cannot afford to "Leave No One Behind". There are research efforts in Uganda to revive the conservation of traditional food systems particularly vegetables. Covid-19 provides an opportunity of how we should treat nature differently. Indeed, time for nature – is now.

*Nagginda is the Nnaabagereka of Buganda.*

Daniel Kalinaki
t Vuchiri-Alumai

29/35 8th Street, P.O. Box 12141
Kampala, Uganda

Phones 0312301100/101
Fax 0412232369

Email editorial@ug.nationmedia.com
Registered at the GPO as a newspaper

---

**20 Bukedde** Lwokubiri, December 14, 2018 **MASAKA**

# Gavt. erwanyise eky'abawala abato abafuna embuto - Nnaabagereka

Bya JOANITA NAKATTE

# Nnaabagereka banaamuyamba okutumbula embeera z'abantu

Bya LILIAN NALUBEGA
NE MOSES KAWALYA

LILIAN NALUBEGA

Katikkiro Mayiga, Cherie Blair ne Nnaabagereka eggulo e Mmengo.

MUKYALA WEYALIKO Katikkiro wa Bungereza Cherie Blair alambudde ebikolebwa ekitongole kya Nnaabagereka ekya Naabagereka Development Foundation mu kaweefube w'okulaba ng'ekitongole kye ekya Cherie Blair kisobola okukolagana nakyo okutumbula embeera z'abantu.

Cherie Blair eyatuuse ku Bulange ku ssaawa 3.00 ez'oku makya yaya-niriziddwa Katikkiro Charles Peter Mayiga ne baminisita ba Kabaka, Nnaabagereka n'abakungu ku lukiiko lwa Nnaabagereka Development Foundation, n'olukiiko olufizi n'oluvannyuma n'agenda mu ofiisi ya Nnaabagereka gye baasoose ne boogeraganya.

Yalambuziddwa olukiiko lwa Buganda n'amayonnyobwa n'ebyafaayo byalwo ng'eno gye yavudde n'atuukako mu ofiisi ya Katikkiro eyamunnyonnyodde enteekateeka y'obululembeze bw'Obwakabaka bwa Buganda gye yagamiye nti ekola kinene mu kubanyinnizaawo.

Nnaabagereka yayingiza abagenyi be mu kisenge ekiteesezebwaamu baminisita ba Kabaka ekyo kabineti gye yidegeezeza Cherie nga bwe yatandikawo NDF ng'alambirira okutumbula embeera z'abantu mu byobulamu, ebyenjigiriza, okutumbula embeera z'abaana, abavubuka n'abakyala.

Yagambye nti mu nteekateeka eno akoze ebintu bingi omuli okunnyikira ennono n'obuwangwa mu buntu abato ate n'okukabafudde abantu ab'omugaso mu bulamu bwafwe obw'omu maaso ng'ayita mu nteekateeka ey'ekisaakaate mw'agunyiilde kati abaana abasoba mu 6,000.

Cherie mu kwogera kwe yategeezezza nti ekitula yuze kula ba en-teekateeka n'enkula y'ekitongole kya NDF n'okutumula engeri gy'ayinza okukolagana nakyo okutumbira embeera z'abantu.

Yannyonnyodde nti yatandikawo Cherie Blair Foundation CBF n'ekigenderererwa cky'okuyamba abakyala abaliko emirimu gye bakola okufulaakulanya amawanga nga n'ekikulu kwe kubiwa obukugu mu ndinikanya y'emirimu gyabwe, engeri y'okwegamfikaanu teknnologya, okukwataganamu n'abantu ab'enjawulo mu mirimu gye bakola.

Katikkiro Charles Peter Mayiga yasiimye enkolagana ya Nnaabagereka ne Blair ate n'Obwakabaka n'amusaba bw'anaaba akomyewo bongere okuweebwa omukisa bamu-manyise ebikwata ku Bwakabaka.

# Blair, Nnabagereka partner to empower women

By Jeff Andrew Lule

It was a colourful function as the Nnabagereka Sylvia Nagginda hosted Mrs. Cherie Blair, wife of the former British prime minister at Bulange, Mengo on Monday.

After they were received by the Katikkiro, Charles Peter Mayiga at 9:30am, Mrs. Blair and her delegation were treated to a Buganda cultural dance.

The Nnabagereka joined her guests and led them to her office, where they had private talks for over an hour.

The press were later ushered into the boardroom for a briefing. The event was attended by several Buganda Kingdom officials and the Nnabagereka Development Foundation (NDF) management.

A jolly Nnabagereka said it was an honour to host Mrs. Blair at the Buganda Kingdom headquarters and emphasised that (NDF) will closely work with the Cherie Blair Foundation for Women (CBFW) to uplift livelihoods of women in the kingdom and the country at large.

"I have seen you supporting many women in different African countries like Rwanda and Nigeria and I believe this is a great opportunity for Uganda since both organisations have the same vision of changing the lives of grassroots women for the better," said the Nnabagereka.

She stressed that NDF focuses on using culture as the vehicle to change the lives of women, youth and children by empowering them socially and economically.

Nnabagereka said the kingdom has the ability to fundraise for the communities or resources necessary for development.

NDF has over 50,000 female members who are supported to achieve sustainable economic independence through savings, and adding value to their produce and commodities.

The Nnabagereka, highlighted the youth camp dubbed "Ekisakaate" (cultural camp), which has been running for nine years as one of the most effective approach for cultural grooming. This is where leadership and other social skills are imparted to children.

She said over 6,500 children have benefited from this project.

Mrs. Blair commended the Nnabagereka for her commitment to uplifting the livelihood of women in the kingdom.

She said she is going to design a plan on how the two organisations will partner and facilitate various projects. This will enable the 50,000 members in NDF benefit from the numerous trainings.

She stressed that loans and savings is the surest way of alleviating people from poverty. However, she asserted that this can be achieved if women acquire entrepreneurship and financial literacy training.

The Cherie Blair foundation for Women supports women entrepreneurs in Africa, South Asia and the Middle East.

"The Nnabagereka is a big inspiration to Buganda. Your visit re-energises us and gives us confidence that NDF's track is not in vain; send our warm greetings to Mr. Tony Blair and tell him we appreciate his work," said Mayiga.

He added that Mrs. Blair's visit was an honour to the kingdom. He expressed his appreciation towards the commitment undertaken by Mrs Blair to partner with NDF and Buganda Kingdom.

Cherie Blair, known professionally as Cherie Booth, is a British barrister.

Buganda prime minister Mayiga, Cherie Blair, the Nnabagereka of Buganda Sylvia Naginda and Buganda government officials during Cherie's visit to Bulange, Mengo. Photo by Miriam Namubebi

SUNDAY SPORT
www.newvision.co.ug

🖪🖿 45
Sunday VISION, July 19, 2015

# NABAGEREKA EXCITES TEAM

PICTURE BY SAMSON OPUS

Nabagereka of Buganda Sylvia Nagginda sparked off a wave of excitement as she visited the Special Olympics camp in Kampala on Friday. The Nabagereka, who is also the patron of Special Olympics Uganda, wished the team success at this year's games due July 25-August 3 in the United States. The team will compete in athletics, swimming, open water swimming, football and volleyball at the world's top sports show for children and adults with intellectual disabilities. The event in the United States will have athletes from 177 countries

**NEXT** REVISITING KIDEGA'S JOURNEY TO EALA SPEAKERSHIP

TRUTH EVERY DAY

# Daily Monitor

CULTURE: CHILDREN'S ANNUAL HOLIDAY CAMP ENDS. P3

# Why African youth matter in environmental discourse

## SYLVIA NAGGINDA NNABAGEREKA

# Nnabagereka asabye abantu okugaba omusaayi

**By DICKSON KULUMBA**

Nnabagereka nga yeetabye mu kaweefube w'okugaba omusaayi ku Bulange - Mmengo.

**Bya DICKSON KULUMBA**

NNAABAGEREKA Sylvia Nagginda asabye abantu bonne okukolera awamu okukunnyaanya omusaayi okumalawo ebbula lyagiwo eriваako abantu 20 buli lunaku okufa mu Uganda. Ku bano 18 babeera balyaala abazaala.

Bino yabyogeredde Bulange - Mmengo ku Lwokubiri ng'atongoza enkola y'okugaba omusaayi okugunda olowetoolola amasaza gonna mu Bwakabaka bwa Buganda.

"Nga mkoledde wamu tusobola okukunnyaanya omusaayi ebitundu 80 ku buli 100 ku musaayi ogwetaagibwa. Obwetaavu bw'omusaayi mu malwaliro bwa nnanyi wadde Kabaka Foundation ne Redcross babadde bakunnyaanya omusaayi buli mwezi," Nnaabagereka bwe yategeerezza.

"Enteekateeka eno ejja kuyamba okwongera obungi

bw'omusaayi ate n'okukendeeza omuwendo gw'abantu abafa obw'ebbula ly'omusaayi noolwekyo nkubiriza mwenna okutwegatako okukunnyaanya omusaayi ogwetaagisa," bwe yagaseecko.

Minisita w'ebyobulamu, Dr. Prosperous Nankindu yabutelidde abantu nti okugaba omusaayi kuhingi eri obulamu era n'obusaba n'okwemanyiiza okulya n'okunywa obulungi.

Christopher Bwanika, Ssaabawolereza wa Buganda era Minisita wa gavunenti ez'ebitundu yategeezezza ng'ensangi zino okwekoona kw'omusaayi bwe kusse abantu abangi nnye ng'okugaba omusaayi kuyamba okumalawo kino.

Edward Kaggwa Ndagala, akulira Kabaka Foundation ne Irene Nakataka baategeezezza ng'ebitongole byonna bwe biri ebimalirivu okukunnyaanya omusaayi okuyamba Bannayuganda.

**18** **Bukedde** Ssande February 4, 2018 **Yiga Olugan**

# Okukuuma n'okunyweza omukwano mu Buganda

Nnaabagereka wa Buganda Sylvia Nagginda ng'asala keeki n'abaana.

**MARIAM KYABANGI**

SSANDE ewedde twatunuulidde okuyisa obulungi omuliraano ng'obumu ku buvunaanyizibwa bw'omuzzanganda. Olwaleero nga tuwumbawumba olugendo lwaffe ku nkola y'ekizzanganda, katutunuulire omukwano.

Omuntu omulamu abeerako n'emikwano gye kumpi mu buli kkoŵe lya bulamu bwe. Abawi b'amagezi, ab'ebinyumu, aboomunda, n'abalala. Abaganda kigambo mukwano baakitwala wala ddala okutuuka ku ssa ly'okutta omukago ogwafuulanga aboomukwano abooluganda! Olaba baagera n'engero nga: 'Omukwano gusinga oluganda!'

Mu kulafuubanira okukuuma n'okunyweza omukwano, Abaganda baakolanga ebintu bingi omuli: okutoneragana, okwetonderagana, okusonyiwagana, okuyambagana mu buli mbeera n'okukuumiragana ebyama ng'ebiraamo.

Zino wammanga ze zimu ku ngero ensonge ezikkaatiriza obukulu bw'okukuuma n'okunyweza omukwano:

**1. Akatono ke kazza omukwano.**

Olugero luno lutegeeza nti bwe wabeerawo okusoowagana wakati w'aboomukwano, akantu akatono kasobola okuzzaawo enkolagana. Okugeza akalabo.

**2. Waggumbulizi k'aba nako, k'awa munywanyi we.** Luno lutegeeza nti abantu aboomukwano buli omu ky'aba nakyo ne bwe kiba kitono ky'awa mukwano gwe. Lutuyigiriza butalinda kumala kubeera na bingi okugaba.

**3. Ekitentegere gye bakyagala, gye bakyalirira omusala.** Ekitentegere lwe lubugo olubi, omusala lwe lubugo olulungi. Bw'olaba omuntu ayalirira ow'ekitentegere n'omusala, ddala abeera anwagala okukamala. Lutuyigiriza kwagala nnyo abo be twagala, mu mbeera yonna gye baba balimu.

**4. Nditwala kinene, afa tatuuse ku buko.** Luno lutegeeza nti omuntu bw'alinda okumala okufuna ebingi alyoke agende atone eri abo abamuvunaanyizibwako ng'abako, aboolaganda, n'emikwano ayinza obutatuuka.

Lutuyigiriza okulaga abo be twagala ne be tulinako obuvunaanyizibwako okwagala nga tubawa ebyo ebitono bye tuba nabyo mu kiseera ekyo. Ebyobulamu munnange tomanya! Leero w'oli, enkya toliiwo.

**5. Tunaalaba, ye kojja w'abakodo.** Luno lutegeeza nti omuntu omukodo takumma butereevu wabula akunguyaaguya na kukugamba nga bw'anaalaba, okutuusa lw'okivaako. Embeera eno nsaale mu kusattulula enkolagana anti omuntu oyinza n'okumuliisa amabanja ng'asuubira nti olina ky'ojja okumuwa. Lutuyigiriza kwogera kituufu okusinga lw'oteeka mu muntu essuubi ate n'otatuukiriza!

# SYLVIA NAGGINDA:
## A QUEEN TOUCHING THE NATION'S VERY SOUL

By Gumisiriza Mwesigye
Published on September 7, 2012 by *The Monitor*[1]

---

## THE NNABAGEREKA OF BUGANDA:
## THE DRIVE BEHIND GIRL CHILD EDUCATION IN UGANDA

Written by Catherine Akurut (1)
Published on February 02, 2012 by *Consultancy Africa*

---

## BUGANDA KINGDOM'S QUEEN MOTHER NABAGEREKA
## SYLVIA NAGGINDA TALKS ABOUT HER LIFE PASSIONS

By Walakira Nyanzi
Published on February 21, 2014 by *We Informers*[2]

If you asked many Ugandans who is their model woman, many will tell you, "the Nabagereka". Readers of Uganda's leading newspaper have always voted Nabagereka Sylvia Nagginda the best woman of the year in the newspaper's annual polls of the best and the worst.

---

1.  https://www.monitor.co.ug/uganda/special-reports/uganda-50/sylvia-nagginda-a-queen-touching-the-nation-s-very-soul-1525134, accessed on Jan 31, 2023
2.  http://weinformers.com/, accessed on January 31, 2023

# CULTURE KEY IN CHILD UPBRINGING – NAGGINDA

By Apollo Mubiru
Published on June 10, 2019 by *New Vision*[3]
Nagginda challenged parents to take their role as the first teachers to their children saying this gives their children a good foundation.

The Nnabagereka of Buganda Sylvia Nagginda at the Royal dinner to launch Ekisaakaate in Manchester (Courtesy photo)

# NABAGEREKA SPEAKS OUT ON CHILD SEX

The Nabagereka of Buganda, Sylvia Nagginda. PHOTO/File newvision
By Anne Mugisa in Addis Ababa
Published on November 15, 2013 by *New Vision*[4]

3.  https://www.newvision.co.ug/news/15016/1/culture-key-child-upbringing-nagginda, accessed on January 31, 2023
4.  https://www.newvision.co.ug/new_vision/news/1334599/nabagereka-speaks-child-sex, accessed on January 31, 2023

# NNABEGEREKA LAUNCHES SEVENTH KISAAKAATE

The Nnabagereka of Buganda Kingdom Sylvia Nagginda waves to the pupils of Green Hill Academy during the launching of the seventh youth camp at Bulange Mengo Headquarters in Kampala on September 17, 2014. PHOTO/ Francis Emorut newvision

By Francis Emorut
Published on September 18, 2014 by *New Vision*[5]

# PUT SANITATION FIRST! NNABAGEREKA URGES WOMEN

The Nnabagereka of Buganda, Sylvia Naginda Luswata – in the company of the Kabaka Ronald Mutebi – has urged women to emphasize sanitation in their homes. (PHOTO/Namajja)

By Elizabeth Namajja
Published on May 9, 2019 by the *PLM Daily*[6]

---

5. https://www.newvision.co.ug/new_vision/news/1310204/nnabege-reka-launches-seventh-kisaakaate, accessed on January 31, 2023
6. https://www.pmldaily.com/features/health/2019/05/put-sanitation-first-n-nabagereka-urged-women.html, accessed on January 31, 2023

# WE NEED MORE GIRLS AND WOMEN LEADERS - NABAGEREKA

Nabagereka Slyvia Nagginda with students during the launch of the Girl's Leadership Academy youth conference dubbed "Wats up" at Hotel Africana. Photo by Juliet Lukwago newvision

By Juliet Lukwago

Published on April 04, 2014 by *New Vision*[7]

7. https://www.newvision.co.ug/news/1339353/girls-women-leaders-naba-gereka, accessed on January 31, 2023

Made in the USA
Middletown, DE
23 February 2024

50218134R00179